Praise for *The Lc*

MW01059045

"*The Longing in Between* is a woɪĸ ᴜɪ sheer beauty. Many of the selected poems are not widely known, and Ivan M. Granger has done a great service, not only by bringing them to public attention, but by opening their deeper meaning with his own rare poetic and mystic sensibility."

ROGER HOUSDEN
author of the best-selling *Ten Poems to Change Your Life* series

"Ivan M. Granger's new anthology, *The Longing in Between*, gives us a unique collection of profoundly moving poetry. It presents some of the choicest fruit from the flowering of mystics across time, across traditions and from around the world. After each of the poems in this anthology Ivan M. Granger shares his reflections and contemplations, inviting the reader to new and deeper views of the Divine Presence. This is a grace-filled collection which the reader will gladly return to over and over again."

LAWRENCE EDWARDS, PH.D.
author of *Awakening Kundalini: The Path to Radical Freedom*
and *Kali's Bazaar* (as Kalidas)
www.thesoulsjourney.com

"I have long thought that poetry offered the deepest most imaginative theology, coming as it does from the heart and the soul, rather than the analytical mind. Ivan M. Granger has woven these poems into a tapestry of great wisdom with his reflection on each poem. I can imagine each poem and commentary furnishing the basis for a daily meditation. I would recommend this anthology to lovers of poetry, to mystics, and to explorers of the spiritual life."

HARVEY GILLMAN
author of *Consider the Blackbird*
and *A Light that is Shining: An Introduction to Quakers*

"Having finished *The Longing in Between* I now feel like a dry field might feel after several hours of being drenched by a gentle, steady rain. This beautiful book is a love letter to and from the Beloved. I was as moved by Ivan M. Granger's commentaries as I was by each poem. As well as sharing a unique collection of sacred poetry, he invites the reader into his inner sanctum, where he reveals the depth of his personal journey, by sharing his insights on each poem."

RASHANI RÉA
artist and author of *Beyond Brokenness*

"One thing I love about *The Longing in Between* is how inclusive this book is. What is different here is that Ivan M. Granger's heart is not only open—it's made deep from spiritual practice; and with increasing depth comes a greater clarity. Nothing is forgotten or overlooked; virtually everything that delivers a vibration of the sacred shows up on these pages.

"The other thing I love is how Ivan M. Granger unfolds each poem with equal attention. Everything matters. This equal attention informs me not only about nuances and details, mysteries and questions that might slip by my reading, but through Ivan's reflections I learn about respect, and gain a much greater respect for—and love, yes, love for the longing in between."

JOHN FOX
The Institute for Poetic Medicine
author of *Poetic Medicine: The Healing Art of Poem-Making*
and *Finding What You Didn't Lose*

"Through his gifts as a poet, anthologist and spiritual seeker, Ivan M. Granger makes a timely, beautiful contribution to our personal spiritual experiences and to our collective thinking. He is highly tuned to our most profound yearnings, answering them with rare grace and always at the service of the words he is sharing. *The Longing in Between* will bring much joy, consolation and insight to all who rest in its pages."

REV. DR. STEPHANIE DOWRICK
author of *Seeking the Sacred, Heaven on Earth*
and *In the Company of Rilke*

"*The Longing in Between* is a treasure house chock full of precious poetic gems which will thrill and inspire the reader, and lead him or her on to a greater understanding of life's spiritual mysteries and miracles. It could well prove to be a life-changing event for anyone who loves and enjoys what Shelley called 'The Higher Poetry.' This book is a 'Bedside Dipper'—each morning a page can be opened and read for an illuminating day, and at night to inspire auspicious dreams. *The Longing in Between* should adorn every library shelf, where it will well deserve an honoured place."

ALAN JACOBS
author and editor of *Poetry of the Spirit: Poems of Universal Wisdom*

Praise for *Real Thirst*

"I found *Real Thirst* to be a slow, cool and refreshing drink. I believe you will find these poems an antidote to the rush of your days."

JOHN FOX
The Institute for Poetic Medicine
author of *Poetic Medicine: The Healing Art of Poem-Making*
and *Finding What you Didn't Lose*

"Every page of this book is a luminous portal through the details of this world into the vastness of pure being. I will turn to these poems again and again for transport to the ineffable, for medicine to heal my restless mind, for a fierce and tender dose of the Beloved."

KIM ROSEN
author of *Saved by a Poem: The Transformative Power of Words*

The Longing in Between

Sacred Poetry from Around the World
A Poetry Chaikhana Anthology

Edited with Commentary by
Ivan M. Granger

POETRY CHAIKHANA

www.poetry-chaikhana.com

ISBN: 0985467932
ISBN-13: 978-0-9854679-3-7

For our hidden teachers,
those we've never met,
and those we meet daily.

CONTENTS

INTRODUCTION

a star

a tree

and the longing in between

réalta

crann

is an tnúthán eatarthu

Gabriel Rosenstock

Without even formulating a complete sentence, Irish poet Gabriel Rosenstock gives us the whole spiritual endeavor—rootedness and aspiration, life, light, a terrible void, and the aching heart that impels us onward.

The longing in between...

Each poem in this collection is born of that same longing—the crisis of separation and its resolution.

If longing poses the question, then union is the answer.

This vibrant tension between longing and union reminds me of a story told by the 10th century Persian Sufi master Junayd. When asked why spiritually realized masters weep, he responded by telling of two brothers who had been apart for years. Upon their reunion, they embraced and were filled with tears. The first brother declared, "What longing!" to which the second brother replied, "What joy!" Longing and fulfillment, the one is not separate from the other.

The mystic maps the territory between the soul and God, between lover and Beloved, between the little self and the true Self, between the transitory and the Eternal. The road connecting these is the road of longing. Mysticism is the science of longing.

The poems gathered in these pages speak to us of seeking and awakening... and the longing in between.

The Language of the Soul

Mystics write poetry, universally. Saints and sages, shamans and seers, wise women and medicine men—they sing songs, they riddle, they rhyme.

Numinous experiences are not easily communicated through words. The sacred can be witnessed and participated in, but not conveyed through limited concepts. Any attempt to communicate what is perceived in states of encompassing unity and mental quiet is necessarily an act of translation. Prose is a poor medium for the task. Its descriptive language works best with known definitions and accepted meaning. Prose is a language of boundaries. Yet the most profound experiences refuse to be contained.

Poetry, on the other hand, does not define; it suggests. Where prose describes, poetry allows meaning to gather. It is this elastic nature that makes poetry well suited to the sacred, enabling language to relay truth without circumscribing it.

Sacred experience is beyond word and form, yet the limited mind, in trying to understand what it has witnessed, reflexively interprets its experience in terms of the world known to the senses. What emerges is a primal language of metaphor, a rich and spontaneous pidgin that develops between the limited mind and the unlimited awareness.

Bliss, perceived through the senses as sweetness upon the palate, evokes the taste of honey. The mystic's trembling ecstasy, accompanied by the sense of imbibing an ethereal drink, leads to language of wine and drunkenness. Profound stillness and the perception of an all-pervading light paints before the mind's eye scenes of the full moon glowing quietly above the resting landscape at midnight. The fiery rising of the *Kundalini* paired with the loss of ego inspires verses on the moth's ecstatic annihilation in fire.

Regardless of culture and religious tradition, mystics everywhere fill their songs with these same metaphors.

In mundane perception, when everyone and everything is seen as separate and isolated, at most one can speak in simile, recognizing that one thing is like another. In that mind-set, metaphor is merely artistic pretense. But to the seer, enraptured by the holistic vision of reality as a fluid interconnectedness, one thing truly *is* another. Metaphor ceases to be a literary device or a dramatic mode of expression; it is observed reality.

It is from this visionary metaphor that sacred poetry is born.

Poetry and Prophecy

A legend is told about Taliesin, the great bard-seer of ancient Wales, of how he stole the "liquid mead of poetry" from a powerful sorceress. The sorceress chased him through a contest of transformations, Taliesin changing form, to be matched by the threatening form assumed by the woman. Taliesin finally took on the form of a single grain of wheat, while the sorceress, becoming a hen, swallowed him—only to give birth to him as a baby in resurrected form. She took the baby, sewed him inside a leather sack, and tossed him into the ocean. But a prince rescued him and gave him the name Taliesin because of his "shining brow" ("tal" means "shining" or "illuminated" in Welsh).

This is, of course, a highly symbolic story. The sorceress is often identified with Ceridwen, the Celtic goddess of death and rebirth who possesses the cauldron of inspiration that is also the night sky. The contest of transformations is the bard's initiation process, the transformation of consciousness and identification with the whole multiplicity of life and the natural world—only then is the poet truly ready to give voice to his verse. And the story of a child thrown into the ocean, the womb of the world, to be rescued by an adoptive parent is a metaphor for rebirth and initiation, variations of which appear everywhere from the Greek myths to the story of Moses.

This tale makes it clear that the bard is not just a wordsmith or musician. No, the poet must go through an ordeal that transforms the awareness and radically expands his sense of self. The poet is expected to be an initiate, a seer, a shaman.

We find something similar in the Icelandic Eldar Edda with the tale of the Norse god Odin. Like Christ, Odin is crucified on a tree, and he is pierced by a stake. He is hung for nine days, a tripling of the three days of Christ's entombment—three and nine, both important numbers of initiation and transformation. Through his suffering upon the tree, Odin is finally given "heavenly mead" to drink, which bestows upon him the divine gifts of wisdom and poetry.

Odin's gift of poetry is not merely the skill to craft words into rhyme; it is the ability to let truth pour unhindered from the deepest core of being and translate that flow into words. The poetry of Odin is oracular, enchanting, infused with magical power.

Poetry, in this sense, is prophecy, relaying the great truths in few words. Poetry transfixes and transforms the listener.

This understanding of poetry—deep poetry—is shared by ancient and traditional cultures all over the world. Just as the Welsh bard may seek *awen* (inspiration, power) by communing with divine forces in a sacred grove, so too does the Zen haikuist take to the road seeking that moment of *satori* (insight) that will unlock the depth of his art. The Taoist poet retreats to the cloud-covered mountains. The Shiva poet finds a secret cave. The Sufi makes his *Hajj*, losing more of himself with each step of the journey. The Christian monk disappears into his cell and learns to fathom the depths he discovers there. Only then is one ready to write poetry.

In this view, true poetry is understood as something beyond the craft of stringing words together, no matter how refined or innovative. Poetry becomes an evocation of the deep awareness. It summons the divine into the daily mind.

This poetry rings with the prophetic voice.

Poets and Mystics

The men and women who composed these poems are poets in the grandest sense—visionaries who sing down the heavens. Some have been acclaimed as saints for their lives of piety and service. But the word "saint" is a loaded one. Some have been called sages for the unique wisdom they've expressed, but a sage might suggest one who is impersonal.

Instead, I tend to refer to these poets broadly as mystics. I prefer this term because a mystic may be a religious figure—of any religion—or entirely secular. A mystic can be a man or a woman. Old or young, educated or uneducated—a mystic may be any of these. To my mind a mystic is someone deeply engaged with the Mystery (of God, of soul, of mind, of self...), without implying anything specific about religion, culture, ethnicity, or gender.

Many mystics are, of course, deeply religious, but they tend to have a unique relationship to their religion. Even the most orthodox mystic is determined to do more than follow the rules and fulfill a pious role. The mystic, by definition, seeks an essential, living awareness of the ultimate reality. While he or she may be a student of theology, ritual, and tradition, the mystic understands them not as absolutes but as signposts pointing the way to direct experience of the Eternal. A mystic, in other words, seeks personal validation of the truths proclaimed by religion and philosophy. Determined to walk the path and not simply read about it, mystics test and question with each step. As a result, mystics make poor dogmatists. But they make excellent poets.

—◦◦◦—

Commentary

The style of my commentary is conversational and idiosyncratic, expressing my personal thoughts and experiences—with occasional tangents and esoteric ramblings. It is my hope that this fluid, non-academic approach will invite you into your own meditative exploration of these poems.

I believe that a poem, like a dream, has layers of meaning, and that its meaning can shift over time and when viewed from different perspectives. My thoughts are offered to suggest a possible starting point of understanding or, perhaps, as a way to begin forming your own relationship with each poem. What I have to say about a poem is not its definitive meaning.

Sacred poetry is transformative poetry. No matter how much we think we have understood, until we feel a poem working its alchemy on our own awareness, we haven't yet met the heart of the poem. So, as you read these poems, discover your own moments of insight and let them work their magic on you!

1
Slowly Green

Bring all of yourself to his door:

Bring only a part,
and you've brought nothing at all.

Sanaí

IMG

Bring all of yourself ∿

These few lines get to the essence of spiritual seeking. What does it mean to bring all that we are to God's door? How do we stand fully before the Eternal Presence? This is the fundamental dilemma faced by every seeker.

The truth is that we are always before the Eternal Presence, but most of the time we are not aware of what is happening. The problem is not that God isn't there; it's that we are not there. Not fully. What then does it mean to bring all of ourselves to that meeting?

Striving to be fully present, we wrestle with our own reflexes, trying to bring our whole selves to the threshold—and yet we hold back.

We each have a deep-seated instinct to hide. We feel protected when hidden. To be unseen is to be safe. This is the entire purpose of the ego, to create a social mask behind which to hide ourselves. We gather our experiences, stitch them together with a narrative, and present that patchwork creation to the world, saying, "This is me. Look no further." The formulation and modification of this ego-mask becomes the primary work of our lives, and we too easily forget that we are not that mask. We forget that we are, in fact, something much larger and less easily defined. The act of hiding becomes institutionalized in the awareness. Only a rebellion can overcome this entrenched pattern. But before that revolution can catch fire and spread throughout the psyche, we need to recognize the effects of this dynamic and we have to truly decide that we want to hide no more.

Now, we need to be clear with ourselves that there may very well be reasons to present a specific image of ourselves in social situations. Some parts are emphasized and others necessarily held back. Some aspects of our lives are appropriately private or sacred or vulnerable, and not to be casually shared.

Here's the thing: That same valid self-protection mechanism becomes spiritually toxic when we try to hide aspects of ourselves from our own awareness... or from God. We need to drop those fig leaves that were a naïve attempt to hide from the All-Seeing.

The fullness of all that we are is much bigger than any story we seek to fold it into. We cannot truncate parts of ourselves to force a snug fit inside the story we want to tell. We must dwell in our entirety. Anything less becomes self-dismemberment. We must claim all of our history, all our feelings and thoughts, the painful and the celestial, all together.

And then we step up to the threshold. Hesitant, naked, vulnerable, we step up to God's door. We enter the eternal present moment. That's when the magic happens. The large, unwieldy collection of victories and wounds we've brought with us comes into focus for the first time and we have a vision of ourselves, our whole selves, alive and immense, integral within the living immense universe. That which we were hesitant to look at within ourselves becomes an image of beauty and, yes, majesty, blissfully melting into the majestic Beauty all around us.

We all, at some level, crave this encounter precisely in order to heal the deep pain of separation. If we come with less than our whole selves, if we come with only fragments of our being, how then can we find healing?

Bring all of yourself to his door

—ᴧ᷎᷎ᴧ—

even poorly planted
rice plants
slowly, slowly… green!

Issa

English version by David G. Lanoue

Even poorly planted ∼ᴑ

There is something healing about this haiku.

These words suggest to me that no matter how imperfect we imagine our circumstances to be—lack of education, finances, travel, guidance, whatever we think is missing and holding us back—still we inexorably grow green. Spirit awakens in us with utter disregard to the limiting details of our lives. And what is truly beautiful is the unique ways that greenness comes upon us. The story we get to share with the world is the specific way that spirit rises in us, the special path it finds around the obstacles that make up our individual lives, and how we are often strengthened by this navigation.

While daily life itself may have its challenges and struggles, that greening process, well, it just happens—slowly, patiently, naturally. All we have to do is let it.

—⌒⌒⌒—

Dark young pine, at the center of the earth originating,
    I have made your sacrifice.
    Whiteshell, turquoise, abalone beautiful,
    Jet beautiful, fool's gold beautiful, blue pollen beautiful,
    Red pollen, pollen beautiful, your sacrifice I have made.
    This day your child I have become, I say.

    Watch over me.
    Hold your hand before me in protection.
    Stand guard for me, speak in defense of me.
    As I speak for you, speak for me.

        May it be beautiful before me.
        May it be beautiful behind me.
        May it be beautiful below me.
        May it be beautiful above me.
        May it be beautiful all around me.

        I am restored in beauty.
        I am restored in beauty.
        I am restored in beauty.
        I am restored in beauty.

Navajo Prayer

English version by Gladys A. Reichard

May it be beautiful 〜

I have come across several variations of this prayer-poem; they all manage to return me to my feet and bring me into quiet awe of the moment.

This version, with its introductory offering to the pine tree is especially moving to me. According to ethnographic notes, this version of the prayer was evoked during healing ceremonies performed in front of a sacred pine tree. The pine tree here is the pillar of life that stands "at the center of the earth," the world navel, the center of being. This pine is the mediator between heaven and earth, a bridge or doorway between the two realms. This is a healing ceremony performed at the point where the sacred and the mundane touch. And that is where we witness the beauty that heals.

I love the evocation: "This day your child I have become, I say." Right relationship is restored. More than restored, it is recognized. The soul uncontracts when it remembers it is the child of something profound, alive, divine... and beautiful.

May you be restored in beauty.

—〜—

A child said *What is the grass?* fetching it to me with full hands,
How could I answer the child? I do not know what it is any
      more than he.

I guess it must be the flag of my disposition, out of hopeful
      green stuff woven.

Or I guess it is the handkerchief of the Lord,
A scented gift and remembrancer designedly dropt,
Bearing the owner's name someway in the corners, that we may
      see and remark, and say *Whose?*

Or I guess the grass is itself a child, the produced babe of the
      vegetation.

Or I guess it is a uniform hieroglyphic,
And it means, Sprouting alike in broad zones and narrow zones,
Growing among black folks as among white,
Canuck, Tuckahoe, Congressman, Cuff, I give them the same, I
      receive them the same.

And now it seems to me the beautiful uncut hair of graves.

Tenderly will I use you, curling grass,
It may be you transpire from the breasts of young men,
It may be if I had known them I would have loved them,
It may be you are from old people, or from offspring taken
      soon out of their mothers' laps,
And here you are the mothers' laps.

This grass is very dark to be from the white heads of old
      mothers,
Darker than the colorless beards of old men,
Dark to come from under the faint red roof of mouths.

O I perceive after all so many uttering tongues,

And I perceive they do not come from the roofs of mouths for
 nothing.

I wish I could translate the hints about the dead young men and
 women,
And the hints about old men and mothers, and the offspring
 taken soon out of their laps.

What do you think has become of the young and old men?
And what do you think has become of the women and children?

They are alive and well somewhere;
The smallest sprout shows there is really no death;
And if ever there was it led forward life, and does not wait at
 the end to arrest it,
And ceas'd the moment life appear'd.

All goes onward and outward—nothing collapses;
And to die is different from what anyone supposed, and luckier.

Walt Whitman

What is the grass? ∾

Why does Whitman give us this prolonged meditation on grass? After all, it is just, well, grass. It is the same green plant surrounding every suburban home, and growing tall in every field and hillside all over the world. We tread on it every day. We know what grass is: it's forgettable.

Not so, says Whitman. We think we know what grass is and remain ignorant. It is easy through familiarity to become blind. We see a lawn, mentally label it as "grass," and never really look or bother to know this plant with which we share so much of the world.

This is what is so startling and refreshing about Whitman's opening line—

> *A child said* What is the grass? *fetching it to me with full hands,*
> *How could I answer the child? I do not know what it is any more than he.*

I love his utterly honest response. Most people presume they know exactly what grass is and can therefore dismiss it from their awareness. But the poet properly sees in the child's fistful of grass a living mystery to be considered.

With Whitman we ask, what is grass really?

It is green hope. It is a handkerchief flirtatiously dropped by God to draw our thoughts to the lovely Face. It is the "babe of vegetation," the embodiment of new life and new growth in the plant world.

What is grass? It is a hieroglyphic, a message layered with hidden meaning. It is a universal teaching encoded in life itself: Like the world's green grasses, we must give generously of ourselves, equally to high and low, without regard to race or nation. Like the grass, it is our nature to grow and to be present, to share our life in every land and landscape.

Then Whitman enters an extended meditation on how grass connects life and death—

12

And now it seems to me the beautiful uncut hair of
*   graves...*
It may be you transpire from the breasts of young men...

Why this gloomy turn? He doesn't just imagine the graves of the elderly who had lived the full measure of their lives, but he sees too the graves of young men and even infants "taken soon out of their mothers' laps." It is important to remember that Whitman is writing in the aftermath of the American Civil War. In fact, during the war, he worked in the New York hospitals. He well knew the bloody reality of young men sacrificed in war.

But here, and elsewhere in his poetry, Whitman makes room even for suffering and violence and death in his philosophy. While he clearly has a compassionate heart, he does not simply label some experiences as unjust, which then must be heroically opposed. Instead, it is as if he watches it all—the beauty and the suffering, everything—unfolding... within himself. It is all him. It is all in the scope of his being. Doing this, he accomplishes a truly courageous feat: integration.

Through that integration, we gain a new vision. We see not life with its end in death, but a living, organic flow of life becoming life becoming life: a perpetual vision of self-renewal. And the grass is the embodiment of this process.

While the dead lie beneath the ground, this green life grows from their now quiet bodies, nourished by their hopes. From the dead comes such pure, delicate new life.

Though there is much to be mourned in Whitman's catalog of the dead, I find the totality of his vision to be reassuring. The grass, the growth of new life, draws even the most premature and unjust deaths into a realm of wholeness and continuity. This vision, which has made room for death, yet understood as part of a greater unfolding of life, welcomes us back into the family of life.

The smallest sprout shows there is really no death

Don't you love that line? And—

13

All goes onward and outward—nothing collapses;
And to die is different from what anyone supposed, and
 luckier.

That last line, every time I read it I am brought to a halt, ready to laugh out loud. What is he saying? "To die is different from what anyone supposed, and luckier."

This whole poem has been his observation on how life renews itself, even through death. But here Whitman seems to be implying something more personal and open-ended, as if his meditation has led him to the notion that death is a sort of initiation into a new and unexpected participation in existence. He has left us with a teasing, Zen-like riddle that offers few answers, yet opens up a pathway of vibrant questions...

—◊—

Sophia in Egypt
(from Three Meetings)

And long I lay in troubled sleep,
Then a whisper: "Rest, friend, rest."
And I slept; and later gently roused—
Earth and sky, the whole world smelled of roses!

Agown in heavenly purple glow you stood,
Eyes full of azure fire,
Your glance was the first blaze
Of world-filling, life-giving day.

What is, what was, what shall forever be—
All, all was held here in one steady gaze…
The seas and rivers blue beneath me,
Distant woods, snow-capped peaks.

I saw all, and all was one—
A single image of womanly beauty…
Pregnant with vastnesses!
Before me, in me—only You.

Vladimir Solovyov

IMG

16

Sophia in Egypt ⁓

Vladimir Sergeyevich Solovyov was a Russian philosopher and poet with an intense connection to the feminine archetype of Sophia or Holy Wisdom. His poem "Three Meetings" was born of a fascinating spiritual adventure. The three meetings referred to in the title are three defining encounters he had with the Divine Feminine, Sophia.

His first meeting occurred at the age of nine, triggered by youthful longings of love for a girl. He lost the girl, and found Sophia.

At the age of thirteen, Solovyov renounced the Orthodox Church he had been raised in and began what he described as a troubled exploration of materialism and nihilism. He initially studied natural history and biology at university, but since his grades began to slip, he switched to studies in history and philosophy.

Sometime about the age of twenty, he "reconverted" to the Orthodox Church, becoming a lay theological student and lecturer. As part of his studies, he traveled to London to do research at the British Museum.

While studying at the British Museum, Solovyov had his second encounter with Sophia. He saw only the Goddess's face this time. Pleading with her to see her full form, Solovyov was told to go and meet her in Egypt.

Solovyov traveled south through Europe and caught a steamer across the Mediterranean Sea, finally arriving in Egypt. He wandered the edges of the Egyptian desert in search of his promised vision of Sophia, but to no avail. Nearly ready to give up, he spent a frigid night in the desert, with the sounds of jackals in the distance. Sophia appeared to him at dawn. He was overwhelmed with a vision of the Earth and of nature, all things, transfigured and unified within the body of the Divine Mother of Wisdom.

> *What is, what was, what shall forever be—*
> *All, all was held here in one steady gaze...*
> *The seas and rivers blue beneath me,*
> *Distant woods, snow-capped peaks.*

Solovyov returned to Russia, becoming an important writer and philosopher who influenced artistic movements and European mysticism in the early 20th century. He advocated an engaged Christianity of service and activism, in which the binding power of Sophia—the maternal wisdom of God—could heal the world. He taught that art could be a modern form of prophecy used to bring greater awareness of this inherent unity to humanity.

> *I saw all, and all was one—*
> *A single image of womanly beauty...*
> *Pregnant with vastnesses!*
> *Before me, in me—only You.*

On many an idle day have I grieved over lost time. But it is never lost, my lord. Thou hast taken every moment of my life in thine own hands.

Hidden in the heart of things thou art nourishing seeds into sprouts, buds into blossoms, and ripening flowers into fruitfulness.

I was tired and sleeping on my idle bed and imagined all work had ceased. In the morning I woke up and found my garden full with wonders of flowers.

Rabindranath Tagore

On many an idle day ∼

These lines from Tagore's *Gitanjali* are addressed directly to God as a sort of a prayer. But Tagore is not asking for something. He is acknowledging a surprising truth: that he sees growth taking place in his "garden" and that it is happening always, secretly, quietly, even when he despairs of his own efforts. He "imagined all work had ceased"—he feels his own spiritual work has come to nothing and his deflated spirit temporarily gives up—but he wakes up surprised to find his "garden full with wonders of flowers."

This is the way of it. Our strivings feel barren and then, unexpectedly, flowers! But why?

The metaphor of a garden to represent spiritual awareness is an ancient one used throughout the world, and it is perfect for what is being said here. Think about a garden for a moment. What is it? First, it is a place where things grow, a place of life. It is the opposite of death, which is the state of non-spirituality. The plants of the garden are rooted in the earth, yet they reach upward toward the light of the sun. At an even subtler level, a garden is a place of nourishment and of beauty. Our spiritual garden feeds us through its fruitfulness. The garden's beauty feeds us too, for it brings the awareness of harmony.

The flowers of the garden represent the spiritual qualities that have opened within us. Those flowers in turn open us to the Divine. The flowers are within us, and we are the flowers. From the yogic point of view, the flowers sometimes represent the *chakra* energy centers that open during spiritual awakening. Also, a garden is a place of contemplation and rest. It is a place where we give ourselves permission to simply be, to settle into the present moment. The garden represents the soul at rest in the living presence of the Divine.

Every plant of the garden grows with a life of its own. The gardener, the spiritual aspirant, may need to till the ground and plant the seeds, water them regularly, keep them free from encroaching weeds—but for all that work, the gardener does not actually make the seeds grow and flower. The gardener just prepares the environment, but it is the divine spark of life "hidden in the heart of all things" that nourishes "seeds into

21

sprouts, buds into blossoms, and ripening flowers into fruitfulness."

Tagore is surprised to realize that his only job is to prepare the garden bed and keep it ready, for the seeds sprout effortlessly. The seeds themselves are alive with the vitality of God. Even when he can conceive of no further effort, the seeds still grow. The seeds *want* to grow. And they will grow. It is in their nature to grow, given the right environment. All we have to do is prepare ourselves, make ourselves ready. The spiritual growth will happen of its own accord. Then one morning we wake up surrounded by "wonders of flowers!"

—∿∿—

The Canticle of Brother Sun

My Lord most high, all-powerful, all-good,
Celebration, light, and all sweet blessings are yours,
        yours alone.
No man speaks
        who can speak your Name.

Praise to you, my Lord, and to all beings of your creation!
Praise especially to brother sun,
        who fills the day with light
        —through whom you shine!
Beautiful and bright, magnificent with splendor,
He shows us your Face.

Praise to my Lord for sister moon
        and for the stars.
You have formed them in the firmament,
        fine and rare and fair.
Praise to you, Lord, for brother wind,
        for the air, for the clouds,
        for fair days and every turn of weather
        —through which you feed the world.

Praise to my Lord for sister water,
        precious and pure, who selflessly serves all.

Praise to my Lord for brother fire,
        through whom you fill the dark with light.
Lovely is he in his delight, mighty and strong.

Praise to my Lord for our sister, mother earth,
        who nourishes us and surrounds us
        in a world ripe with fruit, pregnant
                with grassy fields,
                spangled with flowers.

Praise to my Lord for those seeking your love,
     who discover within themselves forgiveness,
     rejecting neither frailty nor sorrow.
Enduring in serenity, they are blessed,
For they shall be crowned by your hand, Most High.

Praise to my Lord for our sister death,
     the body's death,
     whom none avoid.
A great sadness for those who die having missed life's mark;
Yet blessed are they whose way
     is your most holy will—
Having died once, the second death
     does them no ill.

Sing praises!
Offer holy blessings to my Lord!
In gratitude, selflessly offer yourself to him.

Francis of Assisi

IMG

The Canticle of Brother Sun ～

St. Francis composed his masterpiece, "The Canticle of Brother Sun," in three parts. The first part, in praise of the beauty and holiness of nature, was written in the spring of 1225, immediately following an extended retreat among caves where he is said to have received the stigmata.

The second section, the segment on forgiveness and peace, was composed soon after, perhaps in response to the squabbling of political and religious authorities in Assisi.

The final verses were written late the following year as St. Francis was dying, in which he offers praise to "sister death."

This hymn is one of the first great works written in Italian. At the time, Latin was the language of the Church and of learning. Yet, as part of Francis's humility and affinity with the common people, he composed this praise poem in simple Italian so all could be inspired by it.

Praise for brother sun and sister moon, for the living wind and water and fire and earth. Praise for love and peace, without which the living awareness collapses into barrenness. And praise to death, too, who, in the fullness of time, brings completion and life's final initiation. Through this poem we witness the whole pageant of life expressing itself through us and through all the world.

—◠◠◠—

The Higher Pantheism

The sun, the moon, the stars, the seas, the hills and the
    plains—
Are not these, O Soul, the Vision of Him who reigns?

Is not the Vision He? tho' He be not that which He seems?
Dreams are true while they last, and do we not live in
    dreams?

Earth, these solid stars, this weight of body and limb,
Are they not sign and symbol of thy division from Him?

Dark is the world to thee: thyself art the reason why;
For is He not all but thou, that hast power to feel 'I am I'?

Glory about thee, without thee; and thou fulfillest thy doom,
Making Him broken gleams, and a stifled splendour and
    gloom.

Speak to Him thou for He hears, and Spirit with Spirit can
    meet—
Closer is He than breathing, and nearer than hands and feet.

God is law, say the wise; O Soul, and let us rejoice,
For if He thunder by law the thunder is yet His voice.

Law is God, say some: no God at all, says the fool;
For all we have power to see is a straight staff bent in a pool;

And the ear of man cannot hear, and the eye of man cannot
    see;
But if we could see and hear, this Vision—were it not He?

Alfred Lord Tennyson

The Higher Pantheism ∽

This is a poem worth reading aloud, several times. Listen to the rhythm and the rhyme. Only once you've danced about with the words should you then let the meaning sift in.

Each couplet is rich with insight...

> *The sun, the moon, the stars, the seas, the hills and the*
> *   plains—*
> *Are not these, O Soul, the Vision of Him who reigns?*

I think here the Romantics got it right: To ignore the natural world or merely dominate it, blinds us. It is when we learn to see the living world that we glimpse the underlying reality. This is Tennyson's "Higher Pantheism"—that the Divine is not somehow separate or apart from creation; the Divine is revealed through the living world.

The material world is sometimes said to be a mask or a veil that obscures the Eternal. True enough, but here's the funny thing about masks—they not only hide, they also reveal the contours of the face behind it.

Tennyson invites us to look well, and catch the gleaming eyes peering out through the mask.

> *Dark is the world to thee: thyself art the reason why;*
> *For is He not all but thou, that hast power to feel 'I am I'?*

The world seems like an obstruction only because we ourselves stand in the way of clear seeing. When we recognize our true Self, that which knows "I am I," a stillness and clarity of awareness result. The world is no longer seen as dark and dense and separated, but as an enlightened, interwoven whole.

> *Glory about thee, without thee; and thou fulfillest thy*
> *   doom,*
> *Making Him broken gleams, and a stifled splendour and*
> *   gloom.*

The world all around us—and within us—is filled with a radiant glory, but too often we don't see it. Instead of seeing that shining wholeness, the mind inserts itself into the vision and breaks it apart, dims it, stifles it so the ego can remain unchallenged by something brighter and bigger than itself.

> *And the ear of man cannot hear, and the eye of man*
>   *cannot see;*
> *But if we could see and hear, this Vision—were it not He?*

—⁓—

Within this earthen vessel are bowers and groves, and within
    it is the Creator:
Within this vessel are the seven oceans and the unnumbered
    stars.
The touchstone and the jewel-appraiser are within;
And within this vessel the Eternal soundeth, and the spring
    wells up.
Kabir says: "Listen to me, my Friend! My beloved Lord is
    within."

Kabir

English version by Rabindranath Tagore

Within this earthen vessel ～

> *Within this earthen vessel are bowers and groves, and*
> *within it is the Creator:*

With this verse, Kabir reminds us of the miracle that is this "earthen vessel." The limited earthbound body, together with its interwoven mind, miraculously contains all the "bowers and groves" of creation. And at the center of that garden rests the Creator.

> *Within this vessel are the seven oceans and the*
> *unnumbered stars.*

Within are the "seven oceans," a yogic reference to the seven *chakras* or spiritual energy centers that must be traversed by the awakening consciousness.

> *The touchstone and the jewel-appraiser are within:*

Within is found the "touchstone," that which proves the value of the earthen vessel. And within is found the "jewel-appraiser," the One Who Knows the value of the vessel. The body is a holy object, a priceless treasure, so long as it has been alchemically transmuted by the jewel-appraiser's touch.

> *And within this vessel the Eternal soundeth, and the*
> *spring wells up.*

Within is the eternal sound that hums in silence beneath the noise of the mind. Within is the life-giving spring.

This is a puzzle that the logical mind cannot resolve: the Eternal One, who encompasses all things, is found within the limited compass of the body.

The mystic's voice in ecstasy goads us: "Look within! Look within!"

—〜〜—

33

Such was the Boy—but for the growing Youth
What soul was his, when, from the naked top
Of some bold headland, he beheld the sun
Rise up, and bathe the world in light! He looked—
Ocean and earth, the solid frame of earth
And ocean's liquid mass, in gladness lay
Beneath him:—Far and wide the clouds were touched,
And in their silent faces could he read
Unutterable love. Sound needed none,
Nor any voice of joy; his spirit drank
The spectacle: sensation, soul, and form,
All melted into him; they swallowed up
His animal being; in them did he live,
And by them did he live; they were his life.
In such access of mind, in such high hour
Of visitation from the living God,
Thought was not; in enjoyment it expired.
No thanks he breathed, he proffered no request;
Rapt into still communion that transcends
The imperfect offices of prayer and praise,
His mind was a thanksgiving to the power
That made him; it was blessedness and love!

William Wordsworth

Such was the Boy

This poem may take some extra work before you are drawn in, but it is worth the effort. Sometimes it is easier to read a poem like this aloud. Let the poem's images paint themselves in your mind's eye: a young man standing atop a high hill watching the sunrise illuminate the panorama of earth and ocean spread out before him. This is more than a picturesque moment. Here heaven and earth meet and merge, with the witnessing self at its center.

The boy comes to this encounter raw, wide open. The line, "What soul was his, when, from the naked top..." offers us, along with the boy, a clear view from the promontory. The world lit up and spread out before us is imbibed by our whole being, with nothing filtered out.

Those final lines—

> *Rapt into still communion that transcends*
> *The imperfect offices of prayer and praise,*
> *His mind was a thanksgiving to the power*
> *That made him; it was blessedness and love!*

Standing in awe before the living majesty around us, cast into blissful silence—that is true prayer. The heart, viewing the vastness and diversity of form, the heart opened so wide it witnesses the Formless—that is true prayer.

35

You are all
        the forest

You are all
        the living trees
        in the forest

You are every
        bird and beast
        at play among the trees.

O jasmine lord,
        filling all,
        filled by all,

Where is your face?

Akka Mahadevi

IMG

I really like the image of God (in this case, Shiva) as a forest, as every tree in the forest, and simultaneously as the myriad of animals "at play among the trees."

Contemplate this image for a moment.

First, God is the forest—the place, the region. We might call this the field of being.

But then God is also seen as all the trees—the green and living pillars that collectively embody that field of being. We have shifted from the unmanifest to the manifest.

And then we have the living, moving, "at play" circulation of beings—"bird and beast"—that constantly flows among the trees. Akka Mahadevi is evoking an image of individual points of consciousness playfully moving between the unmanifest and the manifest, between the interior and the exterior. And God is also every one of those points of awareness, circling in and out of manifestation.

We have here an image of God as all life and as all things—all things and, at the same time, flowing through all things... "filling all, filled by all."

It inspires the mystic's plea: "Where is your face?" This vision of unified being within the living multiplicity of beings awakens the soul's fundamental hunger to see it all in a single, welcoming face—for that is the face of our true Beloved and that is the place that is our true home.

—ϖ—

II
Like the Wind Searching

Swallowing
the open field—
pheasant's cry

Yamei

IMG

Swallowing the open field ～

I lived for several years in Hawaii, on the island of Maui. It is a rural island, and I lived "upcountry" amidst the sloping fields and cow pastures. I'd drive my car through the winding country roads of the island, and every once in a while I'd catch a glimpse, from the corner of my eye, of a burst of movement—a pheasant startled from its hiding place. It would ascend with churning brown wings and a sunburst bright head. Then, landing a few yards away, its dignity restored, with its watchful eye once more surveying the yellowing grasses, the pheasant left no doubt as to who ruled that quiet field. One shrill cry confirmed it.

This haiku reminds me of those island moments.

Something about the way Yamei describes the pheasant's cry as "swallowing" the open field, we can almost hear the sharp sound hanging over the field's dewy silence, defining the space. That solitary sound stretching across the empty field, it is a wild cry, an assertion of self, a proclamation of presence and improbable lordship. That single cry casts out a net that draws in the pheasant's whole world, making it his, making it a part of himself. That cry creates union.

And that cry wants to burst forth from your breast too.

—〰—

Chanting, chanting the Beloved's name,
I am myself become the Beloved.

Whom then does that Name
    now name?

Bulleh Shah

IMG

Chanting the Beloved's name ∼

> *Chanting, chanting the Beloved's name,*
> *I am myself become the Beloved.*

We find variations of this statement in sacred poetry and mystic writings throughout the world. What does it mean? How does chanting or repeating the name of the Beloved make one become the Beloved?

A common Sufi practice is *zikr*, the remembrance of the name of God, often through all-night prayer circles that involve passionately repeating the names and attributes of God. We find similar practices in Hinduism and Buddhism with the recitations of divine names and word formulations through *mantra* and *japa*. In Catholicism, there is the repetition of the Rosary. In Orthodox Christianity, there is the Jesus Prayer...

The purpose behind all of these practices is a gentle but persistent assault on the mind. By taking the name or words that most remind us of the Divine, and repeating it over and over again, with attention and devotion, a cleansing process takes place in the awareness. The mind, at first, likes the sense that it is doing something of value, focusing on sacred things; but it soon becomes impatient, wanting to return to its old fixations, its comfortable patterns and habitual ways of viewing the world. Continuing the practice of repetition allows the mind no quarter, bringing it back again and again to focus on the Divine.

Doing this long enough, the mind glimpses empty spaces in itself—a terrifying experience for the mind, since it normally expends great energy to hide its essentially empty nature behind constant activity and attachment.

Continue the practice further still, deeply, and an amazing thing happens: The mind not only sees its emptiness, it sees *through* its emptiness to the radiance within. It recognizes that that shining presence was what was being named all along. And, since the mind has finally admitted that it has no solidity or boundary, that it has no essential reality in itself, it recognizes that there is no separation from that living radiance. The identity is finally understood to have always resided there within the Beloved all along—you have "become the Beloved" yourself!

But, for the devotee, this leaves a dilemma of language: Recognizing the Beloved as one's true self, the Self of all selves, who then shall you call the Beloved? To whom does that Name really point?

This is a verse worth... repeating.

—◇—

Awake! awake O sleeper of the land of shadows, wake!
    expand!
I am in you and you in me, mutual in love divine:
Fibres of love from man to man thro Albions pleasant land.
In all the dark Atlantic vale down from the hills of Surrey
A black water accumulates, return Albion! return!
Thy brethren call thee, and thy fathers, and thy sons,
Thy nurses and thy mothers, thy sisters and thy daughters
Weep at thy souls disease, and the Divine Vision is darkend:
Thy Emanation that was wont to play before thy face,
Beaming forth with her daughters into the Divine bosom
Where hast thou hidden thy Emanation lovely Jerusalem
From the vision and fruition of the Holy-one?
I am not a God afar off, I am a brother and friend;
Within your bosoms I reside, and you reside in me:
Lo! we are One; forgiving all Evil; Not seeking recompense!
Ye are my members O ye sleepers of Beulah, land of shades!

William Blake

Reading Blake's poetry, for me, is like trying to recall a dream that is dense with meaning and feeling. You wade into it knowing that you won't understand it all. You may get lost somewhere along the way. But that is almost beside the point. The goal is to immerse yourself and see what your skin drinks in.

> *Within your bosoms I reside, and you reside in me.*
> *Lo! we are One...*

This poem is God's address to Albion. In Blake's complex mythology, the giant Albion is the embodiment of Britain during its era of colonialism and early industrialism. Blake's God is calling the British nation (we could just as easily substitute the United States or any country) back to its humanity. The Divine Vision has become "darkend" and forgotten. The nation has become a "sleeper of the land of shadows," overcome with "black waters."

To return to ourselves, to awaken, God declares that we must, through love, reconnect to ourselves, to our fellow man, and to the living beauty of the earth.

He gives us a line that echoes:

> *Fibres of love from man to man thro Albions pleasant*
> *land.*

Jerusalem, in Blake's mythology, is a female archetype who is the "Emanation" of Albion. So long as Albion remains asleep, she is hidden. Jerusalem might be understood as the radiant potential of a nation when it throws off its blindness and spiritual lethargy, rising above its hatreds and greed. She is the hidden, divine heart of the nation waiting to emerge.

We each have an individual goal of spiritual awakening, of truly opening our hearts. But Blake reminds us that nations too represent a collective spiritual journey that cannot be ignored. Spiritual awakening is a political act. In truth, it is the fundamental political act because our awareness naturally spreads outward into the wider community.

—~~~—

The Place of Rest

The soul is its own witness and its own refuge.

Unto the deep the deep heart goes,
It lays its sadness nigh the breast:
Only the Mighty Mother knows
The wounds that quiver unconfessed.

It seeks a deeper silence still;
It folds itself around with peace,
Where thoughts alike of good or ill
In quietness unfostered cease.

It feels in the unwounding vast
For comfort for its hopes and fears:
The Mighty Mother bows at last;
She listens to her children's tears.

Where the last anguish deepens—there
The fire of beauty smites through pain:
A glory moves amid despair,
The Mother takes her child again.

AE (George William Russell)

The Place of Rest ~

Several of those phrases resonate in my mind:

> *Unto the deep the deep heart goes...*

> *It feels in the unwounding vast...*

And what a beautiful evocation of the mystic's inner quiet:

> *It seeks a deeper silence still;*
> *It folds itself around with peace,*
> *Where thoughts alike of good or ill*
> *In quietness unfostered cease.*

But I think the final verse is what especially draws my interest:

> *Where the last anguish deepens—there*
> *The fire of beauty smites through pain:*
> *A glory moves amid despair,*
> *The Mother takes her child again.*

At a certain point, the courage to face pain becomes central to spiritual awakening. This is not where we grit our teeth and endure. No, we relax into it. We allow ourselves to truly feel that pain, to yield to it... to accept it. Here's why: The inner pain all experience is ultimately recognized as the (false) perception of one's separation from the Eternal. But that pain itself is the doorway to reunion. By allowing oneself to become completely vulnerable to that pain, to surrender to it, the mystic finds the pain transformed into the blissful touch of the Beloved.

For this reason, mystics and saints describe the pain as being "sweet" or joyful or beautiful... and the path to escape from pain—"there / The fire of beauty smites through the pain."

> *Unto the deep the deep heart goes...*

—∿—

Learning the scriptures is easy;
but living them, that's hard.
Far easier to read words on a page
than to seek the living heart of things.

Stumbling through the fog of study,
I lost my last words—
    and my vision cleared.

    Oh the sight that met me then!

Lalla

IMG

> *Learning the scriptures is easy;*
> *but living them, that's hard.*

All too easily we slip into the bad habit of fundamentalism, confusing the ability to quote scripture and obey rules with actually living the truths they point to. Memorization and carefully controlled behavior don't do the job. That approach never satisfies the heart's urge to open.

But Lalla reminds us:

> *Far easier to read words on a page*
> *than to seek the living heart of things.*

Not only is it unsettling to seek the deeper reality, it is far too messy for the controlling mind. We encounter aspects of ourselves that are frightening and frightened, hidden even from our own awareness. History, hopes, angers, ambitions...

Each human life is far too rich and multi-layered to be truncated into the safe, neat, predefined stories we are told to live out. The human soul is not a cartoon, lacking depth and detail. No, a full spirituality incorporates all that we are. To be holy is to be whole, with nothing left out. The map of the human soul is a topographical map, with mountains and valleys and rivers of life everywhere. Until we've acknowledged that entire landscape, we have an incomplete sense of all that we are and all that humanity is. Because of that patched and incomplete picture of ourselves, compassion collapses, the world appears fragmented, and the vision of the living heart of things is lost in the cracks.

> *Stumbling through the fog of study,*
> *I lost my last words—*
> > *and my vision cleared.*

Recognizing the limitation of memorization and rules, Lalla instead sweeps her mental space clean. Now that is an accomplishment! The real work is not in gathering big concepts or profound thoughts. The truly difficult work is to—let go. When we find the courage to let the lifetime of accumulated words and thoughts fall away, along with the self-important "spiritual" self propped up by them, only then does the fog clear and we finally recognize the spacious selfless self within the wide-open heart.

Instead of just memorizing the words of scripture, Lalla invites us to become the blank page that effortlessly displays them.

Oh the sight that met me then!

———*ᴀᴠᴠᴇ*———

Belief and learning led the way
but failed at Your door.
Only by yielding into Your mystery
was I invited in.

Sanai

IMG

Belief and learning led the way
but failed at Your door.

Personally, I am not a big fan of belief, not in the way most people use it today. I think of belief as the religious equivalent of "fake it 'til you make it." It can help a person go forward when they feel stuck but, let's be honest, there's a certain façade to most of our beliefs.

Belief, we are told, is to trust in something that cannot be proven. The implication is that these are matters beyond our reach as an imperfect individual. It only follows then that we must accept the word of someone else, a spiritual authority, preferably from centuries long past.

I hope it is obvious how that sort of "belief" is inherently flawed. Spiritual knowledge, without direct experience, is just hearsay. Without personal validation, belief is incomplete.

At best, belief can only bring us to the threshold. No matter how loudly or passionately we profess it, belief alone is not enough.

Only by yielding into Your mystery
was I invited in.

The final step—which is really the only step—is the step into the unknown. It is in opening ourselves to the fullness of the sacred mystery all around us that we finally cross the threshold.

True, belief gives some the courage to "yield" and to let the ego disappear in order to step naked through the doorway. But, for too many, belief does the opposite by armoring the ego and becoming the excuse to not see, to not understand, and to not take that step. Those with certainty but no knowledge have little tolerance for the reality beyond their mental scaffolding.

To really meet the mystery we must be uncertain. We must be open-minded, open-hearted, curious, courageous, quiet, poised... and humble enough to not notice our own sweet melting. That is when we've finally stepped through.

—◦◦◦—

My soul,
the way of the masters
is thinner than the thinnest.
What blocked Solomon's way was an ant.

Night and day the lover's
tears never end,
tears of blood,
remembering the Beloved.

"The lover is outcast and idle,"
they used to tell me.
It's true.
It happened to me.

I tried to make sense of the Four Books,
until love arrived,
and it all became a single syllable.

You who claim to be dervishes
and to never do what God forbids—
the only time you're free of sin
is when you're in His hands.

Two people were talking.
One said, "I wish I could see this Yunus."
"I've seen him," the other says,
"He's just another old lover."

Yunus Emre

English version by Kabir Helminski and Refik Algan

> *My soul,*
> *the way of the masters*
> *is thinner than the thinnest.*
> *What blocked Solomon's way was an ant.*

"Thinner than the thinnest," "the way is narrow..." Statements like these make it sound as if the way to real insight demands extremes that few are willing to go to or are even capable of. We assume that every action, every thought, every impulse must be strictly regulated and controlled in order to pass the test and get our *dervish* diploma.

But that's not it. It's not that the seeker must live his or her life as a sort of psychic anorexic, harshly starving away every detail of life. No, the "thinness" of this road is a way of saying that our own sense of self and self-importance must be thinned. The successful mystic must be supremely humble, which can be as easy or as difficult as we choose to make it. Acquiring the necessary humility can be a healing exhalation, a loving embrace of all beyond our boundaries, or it can be a painfully enforced humiliation—our choice.

But supreme humility, that's the key. The inflated self cannot fit through this thinnest way.

> *Night and day the lover's*
> *tears never end,*
> *tears of blood,*
> *remembering the Beloved.*

Tears, blood, pain... Sounds enticing, right? Let's not turn away from this idea too quickly. Here's how I understand this sort of passionate statement: We, all of us, already feel this pain all the time and we have trained ourselves to ignore it. This is the fundamental pain of separation and isolation. As long as we imagine that we are separate from the people we love, the life we desire, the world we hope for, all of which is the feeling of being separate from God or some ultimate sense of Reality—as long as we imagine this separation, we feel pain. That pain is the universal human existential experience. Every relationship, all of society is built on this pain and how we deal with it.

Mystics, being crazy folk, embrace this pain, rather than run from it. To do so is an act of courage and honesty. It is a determination to encounter reality as it is, rather than the comfortable fantasy we want to project. Doing this also develops compassion and empathy for the secret struggles of others.

Perhaps most importantly, embracing the pain of separation opens hard-to-find pathways along the spiritual journey. Surprisingly, the pain itself becomes the doorway to reunion. By allowing oneself to become completely vulnerable to that pain and surrendering to it, the mystic finds the pain transformed into the blissful touch of the Beloved.

In other words, the ache of separation, when viewed with a steady gaze, reveals itself to be a bridge of connection. It doesn't seem logical, but it is true: Yearning is union.

Embrace those tears, but with purpose and confidence, and you will find a hidden joy beneath them.

> *"The lover is outcast and idle,"*
> *they used to tell me.*
> *It's true.*
> *It happened to me.*

"Outcast and idle." I like this phase on several levels. The lover, the seeker, the mystic... why are they outcast? As I mentioned above, they view the world differently, with commitment and honesty and with a determination to see things as they actually are. That makes just about everyone else uncomfortable. The normal state is self-protection and hiding. It's not really that everyone has something to hide, but we instinctively hide anyway. We want so much to be our masks that the steady gaze of someone determined to see honestly frightens us, and we push them away. They become outcasts.

This doesn't mean that the path of the mystic is necessarily one of isolation or lack of connection. It just means that you connect in a different way, hopefully in a way that is ultimately healing for those around you.

The word "idle" here is especially interesting to me. Idle can imply lazy, which the lover is not, or inactive, which might apply in the sense that the lover becomes free from self-will. Action flows through the lover, but doesn't originate with the lover. Or we can say that the lover is idle in the sense of being still and at peace. The lover may or may not be active in the world, but there is a radiating quiet within him and his actions. Idle.

> *I tried to make sense of the Four Books,*
> *until love arrived,*
> *and it all became a single syllable.*

These lines are wonderful.

We can study religious law and tradition, impress those around us with how well we've memorized it and how closely we follow the letter of the law—but what does it really mean? Not much, until divine love bursts from our breast. And then... well, the irony is that we don't need all those words any more. Everything is then resolved into a single word.

> *You who claim to be dervishes*
> *and to never do what God forbids—*
> *the only time you're free of sin*
> *is when you're in His hands.*

Ah, those troublesome mystics. They keep telling us that it's not about rigidly following the rules. The rules don't exist to be followed; they exist to point out a destination. The rulekeepers hate to hear the real truth, that rules, when they work, exist only to help us melt into the embrace of the Beloved. That's the only measure that counts.

> *Two people were talking.*
> *One said, "I wish I could see this Yunus."*
> *"I've seen him," the other says,*
> *"He's just another old lover."*

—⁓⁓—

59

Who has not found the Heaven—below—
Will fail it above—
For Angels rent the House next ours,
Wherever we remove—

Emily Dickinson

Who has not found the Heaven—below—   ~

These four lines by that reclusive American mystic, Emily
Dickinson, proclaim a deep truth:

> *Who has not found the Heaven—below—*
> *Will fail it above—*

This statement has been getting mystics into trouble with
orthodox religious authorities in every century. It is the assertion
that heaven is not found somewhere 'out there'—not in the future,
not after death, not in some celestial otherworld. Heaven is here,
now. It is within us and surrounds us, always! And—the most
dangerous part of this insight—if we don't discover it here
"below," it won't be found elsewhere "above."

A statement like this shatters the religious waiting game, waiting
for death, waiting for the Second Coming (or for the *Maitreya*
Buddha, or for a better rebirth, or whatever...) If the presence of
Christ / Buddha-mind / *fana* / liberation is not recognized right
here where we are, the passive expectation of it coming upon us
some other day, at some other place, is sure to "fail."

Another way of saying this is that, as we discover the heaven
below, we find ourselves already dwelling in the heaven above.
But, on the other hand, if we continue to deny the heaven below,
we'll fail to discover the gateway to heaven above.

Dickinson says, "For Angels rent the House next ours, / Wherever
we remove—" No matter where we go, the Divine Presence is
right there with us. We just have to knock on the neighboring
reality and introduce ourselves...

—*∿*—

One Thread Only

One thread, one thread only!
Warp and woof, quill and shuttle,
countless cloths and colors,

        a thousand hanks and skeins—
    with ten thousand names
    ten thousand places.

But there is one thread only.

Bulleh Shah

IMG

One Thread Only ∾

I imagine a great loom, with colored yarn feeding into it from all directions, the shuttle shooting back and forth, producing a highway of fabric in dazzling patterns and colors.

But obviously Bulleh Shah is talking about more than cloth. When he refers to "ten thousand names / ten thousand places," we recognize he is actually talking about the entire world, all of creation. Bulleh Shah is telling us that, underlying the endless variety and design of the Universe, it is all fundamentally one, made of the same single material.

We look at a multicolored cloth and see green in one part and red in another, and we see these sections as being different. The mind names one "green" and the other "red," and separates them into different categories. We have mentally taken our shears and cut up the cloth—and we then see two where there is, in fact, only one.

It requires a delicate balance of perception to appreciate the endless variety of existence without losing sight of the whole. Most of us learn to pull life's cloth apart into separate swatches. Yet it is only in the interrelated patterns woven across the entire fabric that we witness the grand beauty of the design.

—≈≈≈—

There is no place for place!
How can a place
house the maker of all space,
or the vast sky enclose
the maker of heaven?

He told me:
"I am a homeless treasure.
The world was made
to give you a place to stand
and see me."

Tell me, if the one you seek
is placeless,
why put your shoes on?
The real road
is found by polishing, polishing
the mirror of your heart.

Sanai

IMG

There is no place for place! ∾

I have always loved these lines, but the middle verse particularly stands out to me—

> *He told me:*
> *"I am a homeless treasure.*
> *The world was made*
> *to give you a place to stand*
> *and see me."*

Mystics often declare a fundamental unity in existence. There is no real separation between beings. And there is no separation between the individual and the Eternal.

But this raises a dilemma for the philosopher: In a reality that is all One, why does the perception of separation and multiplicity emerge? Is that simply a false vision, a delusion, or does it serve some divine purpose? In other words, why does that externalized, separate reality we call "the world" come into being?

One way this question is answered is to look at the journey of the individual human consciousness from birth, through individuation, to mature adulthood and, finally, hopefully, to wisdom and enlightenment. As newborn infants we don't imagine ourselves to be separate from our mothers. There is hardly any self at all. Or, rather, self is so open that it is not a "self" in the normal sense. There is only Mother. And the wider reality is only the perception of sensation. This is a form of unity, but it is immature. This initial unity does not yet allow us to effectively interact with the wider, complex reality and embody our full potential.

Next, separation and individuation begins to occur. The toddler discovers a powerful word: "No!" This is a magical assertion of boundaries. A sense of self emerges. This is also when "the world" emerges, understood as a complex reality beyond our personal boundaries. We have become engaged in the game of self and object, self and other.

That self-object dynamic is essential. It allows for interaction. It allows for experimentation and experience and growing comprehension. We gain a vantage point through which to perceive and understand reality. We gain a place to stand and to see.

As necessary as this relationship with reality is, it is ultimately flawed and limited. It works well for the basic need of all beings to figure out how to survive and to socially connect. But it is an incomplete picture, and it leaves us incomplete in ourselves. Even when, as mature adults, we learn the skills of the world, there is a lack. And we know it.

The wise woman or man continues to mature in awareness, rediscovering that primal unity while integrating it with the hard-learned lessons of the world. This leads to true spiritual maturity, with vision and a place to stand, yet consciously connected to all things.

We need the world. We need a place to stand, so we can look and see. Eventually, we once more see the One in the patterns of the many.

Then the idea of place falls away. Place only has meaning amidst the multiplicity, when seeking some segment of reality. But when, in our maturing wisdom, we seek the blissful vision of the Whole Reality, what meaning does place have anymore?

> *There is no place for place!*
> *How can a place*
> *house the maker of all space...?*

Enough running about from place to place; we are on a journey to the placeless. Let's kick off our shoes, sit down, and begin the real work of polishing that most secret center until we truly see, and know, and are whole in that vision.

—◦◦◦—

One shrine to the next, the hermit can't stop for breath.
Soul, get this! You should have looked in the mirror.
Going on a pilgrimage is like falling in love
with the greenness of faraway grass.

Lalla

English version by Ranjit Hoskote

One shrine to the next ～

The pilgrim, rushing from one shrine to the next, tallying up destinations, without pause or reflection, accomplishes little but the loss of breath (or spirit).

Of course, this poem is not just about pilgrimage, it is about how we journey through life. Do we hasten through our experiences without attention? Do we accumulate possessions without purpose? Are we endlessly "in love with the greenness of faraway grass"? In all this breathless hurry, what is it we are really looking for?

That spark, that life, that sense of wholeness—it is never found anywhere outside of ourselves. When we are really paying attention, the outer reflects back to us what was within all along.

We can spend a lifetime looking, traveling, and acquiring. Or we can look in the mirror.

—～※※～—

Every man who knows his secret
becomes a secret,
        hidden from the skies.

The sage says Ahmad rose to the heavens;
Sarmad says the heavens
        rose in him!

Sarmad

IMG

> *Every man who knows his secret*
> *becomes a secret,*
> > *hidden from the skies.*

When we become aware of the secret self contained within us, the surface self disappears. The person most of us imagine ourselves to be has vanished, "hidden from the skies."

> *The sage says Ahmad rose to the heavens;*
> *Sarmad says the heavens*
> > *rose in him!*

Islamic tradition tells of the *Mi'raj*, when the Prophet Mohammed (Ahmad) ascends into heaven, where he converses with other prophets and approaches near to God.

Sarmad, with the mystic's instinct, turns this inward, seeing the *Mi'raj* not as an external journey, but as a journey within, for "the heavens rose in him!" This declaration makes the journey to heaven available to us all. We may not all be prophets, but we all can discover the same heavenly core within.

If we then go back and consider how the two halves of this poem fit together, Sarmad suggests that discovering this "secret" or fundamental truth of reality shifts our relationship with "the heavens." We are no longer held beneath the heavens. Instead heaven is found within us, within an inner spaciousness. This sense of being "hidden," this loss of the little self, also means the loss of limiting boundaries. It is only in this expanded, formless sense of self that we discover the inner pathway to the Divine. Or, you could say, that we discover the heavens as already here, already within us. It is a journey in which we have already arrived.

—⁓—

Friend, this is the only way
to learn the secret way:

Ignore the paths of others,
even the saints' steep trails.

Don't follow.
Don't journey at all.

Rip the veil from your face.

Sachal Sarmast

IMG

Friend, this is the only way ∼

In July 2010, I was driving home from work, listening to BBC news on the radio, and was saddened to hear of a bombing at a shrine dedicated to a Sufi saint in Lahore, Pakistan. More than 40 people were killed and many more badly injured. People speculated that the bombing was by an extremist group that objected to the inclusive nature of Sufi practice in the region.

Islamic extremists have certainly grabbed headlines in recent years, but the world also has its Christian extremists, Jewish extremists, Hindu extremists... as well as plenty of atheist and non-religious extremist groups. Extremism is not a problem of a particular religion; it is a disruption in the human psyche in general.

Religious extremism has very little to do with religion, if you think about it. It is partly a reflexive response to the intensely fragmenting nature of the modern world. And it is partly a reaction against unavoidable, sometimes unsettling encounters with different peoples and cultures and beliefs in our ever more integrated and multi-layered world. But mostly—mostly it is an act of desperation when the heart of true religion has been lost. People become violently obsessed with rules and traditions and texts only when they have lost the sense of what they really point to.

If you know where the Beloved lives, you are content, no need to argue with others over street names. Conflict only arises when you aren't so certain you know the way; that's when another person's map threatens your certainty. Fundamentalism and extremism are an admission of that spiritual uncertainty. Absolutism is not an expression of faith; it is a symptom of the lack of faith. It is a symptom of the lack of true spiritual experience and knowledge.

The real long-term solution to the problem of violent religious extremism in the world is to reawaken that sweet, secret, sacred bliss within ourselves, to gently and generously share it with others, and to create environments nurturing to that continuing quest. The more we fill the world's dry troughs with fresh water, the less likely it is that people will go insane with blind thirst.

—∿∿∿—

Boundless

Like the wind searching,
lifting feathers round
the sparrow's neck,
lifting leaves in a wave
across the bean field,
I find no place
where I can say,
here my being ends.

Colin Oliver

Boundless ⁓

> *I find no place*
> *where I can say,*
> *here my being ends.*

These are the fundamental questions we live our lives asking: Who am I? What am I? What is this experience I call myself?

If I want to know what I am, I also find myself asking what I am not. That is when I must go searching for a boundary. Where does self end and non-self begin?

Searching in this way, a strange thing happens—we find no clear boundary. Yes, we may construct mental maps, proclaiming this is me, and that over there is foreign territory. But then we must protect that limited and, therefore, vulnerable self at all costs. Yet when we actually walk the landscape, we find no fence or lines on the ground. When we choose to see it, the self goes on and on. Each individual is really a magical act of seeing with no fixed eye.

Try to find your boundaries and you will find you are boundless. Imagine the possibilities of being that follow...

—ᴧᴧᴧ—

III
Flood and Flame

E Ho Mai

E ho mai
Ka 'ike mai luna mai e

'O na mea huna no'eau
O na mele e

E ho mai
E ho mai
E ho mai e.

Grant us
knowledge from above,

All the wisdom
of the songs.

Grant,
bestow,
grant us these things.

Edith Kanaka'ole

IMG

E Ho Mai ～

When I lived in Hawai'i, I took a class on *ho'oponopono*. (If you sound it out slowly, it's not the tongue-twister it first appears to be.) *Ho'oponopono* means literally "to make things right, to return things to harmony." It is a traditional healing method, but its emphasis is not on healing the body as much as on healing relationships, families, communities. If you think about it, what is the purpose of a healthy body except as an instrument to work for a healthier society? The small body serves the larger body.

As part of my training in *ho'oponopono*, I learned Edith Kanaka'ole's "E ho mai" chant. Hawaiian chant can be compared to Hindu *mantra*: to say it properly takes training. The inflections are important. The breath is important. Most of all, the sense of personal presence is important.

This Hawaiian chant must be said with force and with heart. It is a prayer, but it is not passive. It is a calling forth, a reaching out and a drawing in—of wisdom, of knowledge, of truth. It evokes in us *pono*, rightness.

Try sounding out the Hawaiian, slowly at first, until the sounds become familiar. Then speak it louder, with confidence. Say it over and over again. Imagine repeating this chant in a group. Let it ring through your body and your day!

Aloha!

—〰—

Bird Bath

only this
matters: this ecstatic
baptism

this standing on stick-
thin legs where the singing
creek pools at the lip
of the waterfall

only this
ruby-feathered
chest diving to meet
its reflection

this beak piercing
again and again that quivering
surface, these wings half-
unfolding, a ruffle

of joy guiding rivers
of light a tumble
of droplets dressed
in rainbows along your hidden
spine

shattering all
decorum beneath
blue branches in quiet

assent...

Elizabeth Reninger

Bird Bath ∿

Isn't this a wonderful poem? We have a distilled moment: a red-breasted bird, a robin perhaps, standing in a creek where the water pools just at the edge of a small waterfall. The bird looks down at its own reflection in the surface, plunges, shaking the water through its feathers. Just an instant of life that happens every day, yet through the poet's eyes it suggests so much to us.

> *...where the singing*
> *creek pools at the lip*
> *of the waterfall*

This isn't in a manmade birdbath, but a creek, with living, flowing water. We are at a precipice, at the edge of a waterfall, and it is there that we find a still point.

Naturally, we identify with the robin. We look down into the stillness right at the edge, and see a reflection of ourselves. With a bold, joyful movement, we dive to meet ourselves, piercing the surface to merge with that other self. In the explosion of the moment, we find life, cleansing, baptism, communion.

> *...these wings half-*
> *unfolding, a ruffle*
>
> *of joy guiding rivers*
> *of light a tumble*
> *of droplets dressed*
> *in rainbows along your hidden*
> *spine*

The poet, being a practitioner of yoga and *qigong*, perhaps intends to suggest the ecstatic rush of *Kundalini* along the spine. Or perhaps simply it is the glistening light and movement of the moment that comes alive in us.

> *shattering all*
> *decorum beneath*
> *blue branches in quiet*
>
> *assent...*

81

I think I like these final lines best of all. Our quiet "decorum" is "shattered" by this moment of life. But reality accepts that disruption, it seems to approve and give its blessing, it offers "quiet assent."

—◦◦◦—

Like a river
        in flood
        filling a dry lake floor,

Like rain
        drenching dried twigs.

An inundation of delight, today,
        the joy of this world
        and the journey beyond—both
Came to me, hand in hand.

O jasmine lord,
        I saw the foot of the holy one today
        and am whole.

Akka Mahadevi

IMG

Like a river in flood ～

You know, there is always a question people are hesitant to ask, or just don't think to ask... So let's ask it now:

Is there anything real behind all of these esoteric poems and sacred writings? Or are these crazy poets and mystics just composing lovely word games built on pointless philosophical speculations?

Here is a little secret not often mentioned in church or mosque or synagogue: In deepest communion, when the mind is still and the heart is open, we are flooded with such an immense, ecstatic joy that nothing else can compare to it.

This bears repeating: When we achieve open-hearted, centered inner quiet, we are flooded with an ecstatic delight beyond description.

It is real.

That flood brings with it a profound sense of life. It is a sense of being alive that is utterly new, unknown until that moment. It is as if we experience what it means to be alive for the first time. Christians speak of this as the rebirth. Eastern traditions speak of it as awakening. That rushing stream slakes a deep thirst we didn't know we had.

> *Like a river*
> *in flood*
> *filling a dry lake floor,*
>
> *Like rain*
> *drenching dried twigs.*

In other words, yes, these poets are actually describing something real. It is something felt and tangible. The spiritual journey is not about withering discipline or theological correctness, clinging to a dusty ideal unto the grave. It is about life! And a deep, mysterious delight!

The theologian reformulates other people's descriptions of sugar and tells himself that he is content. But the mystic is only satisfied with tasting the sweetness.

The spiritual journey is about discovering the very real sweetness
that you are.

> *O jasmine lord,*
> *I saw the foot of the holy one today*
> *and am whole.*

Last night, as I was sleeping,
I dreamt—blessed vision!—
that a fountain flowed
here in my heart.
I said: Why, O water, have you come
along this secret waterway,
spring of new life,
which I have never tasted?

Last night, as I was sleeping,
I dreamt—blessed vision!—
that I had a beehive
here in my heart;
and the golden bees
were making
from all my old sorrows
white wax and sweet honey.

Last night, as I was sleeping,
I dreamt—blessed vision!—
a blazing sun shone
here in my heart.
It was blazing because it gave heat
from a red home,
and it was sun because it gave light
and because it made me weep.

Last night, as I was sleeping,
I dreamt—blessed vision!—
that it was God I had
here in my heart.

Antonio Machado

IMG

Last night, as I was sleeping ∾

This is my favorite poem by the Spanish poet Antonio Machado. Actually, it is one of my favorite poems, period.

> *Last night, as I was sleeping,*
> *I dreamt—blessed vision!—*

The repeated line, which I have translated as "blessed vision," has elsewhere been rendered as "marvelous error." Machado's actual phrase in Spanish is "*bendita ilusión*," but this "illusion" is not an erroneous delusion; it is an illusion in the same sense that a dream or vision is an illusion. It is something intangible, seen and felt but not physically there. I have the feeling that Machado is teasing us by calling the experience a dream, seeing if we are foolish enough to ignore it. Perhaps the poet can't quite believe the beauty of his vision.

Let's take just a moment to explore how this poem parallels the mystic's ecstatic experience...

Machado discovers continual delights in his heart: a flowing fountain, a honey-filled beehive, a blazing sun, God... all found within the heart. Read enough descriptions of mystical union, and the same phrases come up again and again—the heart ablaze with light and heat, filled with sweetness, bubbling and overflowing, a heart expanding to embrace all creation.

> *Last night, as I was sleeping,*
> *I dreamt—blessed vision!—*
> *that a fountain flowed*
> *here in my heart.*

The fountain flows from the heart, running along a "secret waterway." It is a "spring of new life." This is often part of sacred ecstasy. Mystics experience a sensation of drinking some unknown liquid that warms the heart and fills one with a bubbling sense of life previously unknown and unimagined.

> *Last night, as I was sleeping,*
> *I dreamt—blessed vision!—*
> *that I had a beehive*
> *here in my heart;*

The mystic's "drink" is perceived as being sweet, eliciting comparisons to honey or wine. Thus, Machado discovers "white wax / and sweet honey" in his heart.

> and the golden bees
> were making
> from all my old sorrows
> white wax and sweet honey.

In such overwhelming delight one feels radically restored and whole. All past guilts and sorrows seem somehow resolved, transformed into the very matter from which this joy emerges.

> Last night, as I was sleeping,
> I dreamt—blessed vision!—
> a blazing sun shone
> here in my heart.

And the awareness is filled with the perception of a radiant light, while the body is permeated with a great warmth—like a "blazing sun."

Caught up in this experience, how can we doubt that it is God we have inside our hearts?

> Last night, as I was sleeping,
> I dreamt—blessed vision!—
> that it was God I had
> here in my heart.

—⁓—

The Elixir

Teach me, my God and King,
 In all things thee to see,
And what I do in any thing,
 To do it as for thee.

Not rudely, as a beast,
 To run into an action;
But still to make thee prepossessed,
 And give it his perfection.

A man that looks on glass,
 On it may stay his eye;
Or if he pleaseth, through it pass,
 And then the heaven espy.

All may of thee partake:
 Nothing can be so mean,
Which with his tincture (for thy sake)
 Will not grow bright and clean.

A servant with this clause
 Makes drudgery divine:
Who sweeps a room, as for thy laws,
 Makes that and the action fine.

This is the famous stone
 That turneth all to gold:
For that which God doth touch and own
 Cannot for less be told.

George Herbert

The Elixir ～

First, this is a poem that must be spoken aloud. What might seem pleasant, but perhaps a bit bland on the page, takes on a surprising strength when spoken aloud. It has a delightful rhyme that should be savored on the tongue. You need to hear it, not read it.

The title—The Elixir. Elixir is borrowed from Arabic, *al-ikseer*, which can literally translate as "the drink of power." The word "elixir" came into European languages through the medieval fascination with alchemy. ("Alchemy," also an Arabic word.) The elixir is the alchemist's secret drink of immortality. We find similar notions of a sacred drink that confers eternal life in all the world's spiritual traditions. The elixir is also at times referred to as the philosopher's stone, that which true sages use to transforms base metal into gold.

Some alchemical traditions, in both East and West, have pursued the elixir in quite literal, physical terms, seeking a substance that actually changes lead to gold or grants bodily immortality. Other schools understood this language on a more esoteric level, where the immortality found is an immortality of the spirit, in which the base metal of the lower self is transmuted to the gold of the divine Self.

But what is Herbert's elixir? His "tincture" is the inner bliss one discovers when every action is wholly dedicated to God:

> *And what I do in any thing,*
> *To do it as for thee*

This approach "makes drudgery divine." When we put our actions in the context of service to something greater than our own selfish ends, even the smallest task becomes a profound meditation. It becomes a new avenue for spirit to manifest in the world. It becomes a method through which we can know our true nature better.

The results of the action are not the real goal; it is the performance of the action in itself, with proper attention, that is the goal. The outcome is left to God.

Another way to imagine this is that every action, great or small, is a gift offered to the Beloved. When we want to show our love through a gift, we put careful thought into its selection and creation, we wrap it with care and creativity, and we carry it to our loved one's door with a hopeful heart. We do it to give, not to gain. Every action can be the same.

> Who sweeps a room, as for thy laws,
> Makes that and the action fine.

But discovering this elixir through action requires selflessness:

> A man that looks on glass,
> On it may stay his eye;
> Or if he pleaseth, through it pass,
> And then the heaven espy.

Okay, let's reword this for better understanding. We can paraphrase these lines as, "A man who looks in a mirror can stop and stare at himself; or he can pass through his own reflection and then see heaven." This seems to me to be saying that as long as we are fixated on ourselves and on surface appearances, that is all we can hope to see. But when we let go of that self-obsession, move beyond our limited sense of identity and self-ornament, we finally see the real, radiant world of Being.

In other words, we must step out of the way and let the action, whatever it is, flow through us, unhindered by ego or expectation. That's when magic happens. That's when we discover the elixir.

—*∿*—

Thinking

Now that all thoughts have subsided
off I go, deep into the woods,
and pick me
a handful of shepherd's purse.
Just like the stream
meandering through mossy crevices
I, too, hushed
become utterly clear.

Ryokan

English version by Gabriel Rosenstock

Thinking ∼

I really like the way this poem opens...

> *Now that all thoughts have subsided*
> *off I go, deep into the woods,*
> *and pick me*
> *a handful of shepherd's purse.*

Ryokan recognizes how thoughts grow tired of themselves and can finally fall silent. In silence, he enters the woods—a recluse, wrapped in quiet, moving slowly among the trees in search of his simple meal of wild herbs.

This is the part that really awakens:

> *Just like the stream*
> *meandering through mossy crevices*
> *I, too, hushed*
> *become utterly clear.*

He has movement, yes, but it is effortless flow. His entire life at that moment is transparent, completely clear, free from self and the silting of mind.

The poet's entrance into the poem and disappearance into the woods creates a vacuum that draws us in after him. The whole poem is an invitation, leaving us with the question... Shall we, too, slip into the woods?

—⁓⁓—

Not only do the thirsty seek water,
The water too thirsts for the thirsty.

Rumi

IMG

Not only do the thirsty seek water 〜

As I grow older, the idea of spiritual thirst becomes ever more real to me. As a young seeker, in my adolescence and early adulthood, I was consumed by such painful blind thirst that I couldn't have named it "thirst" back then. It was simply the searing ache of my days. It was my whole world.

I went a little mad with thirst. I kept seeking to withdraw—from society, from the world, retreating into the forests of Oregon, the mountains of Colorado, the jungles of Hawaii, where perhaps I might glimpse what was truly essential. I fasted my body into emaciation. I meditated in caves. I walked barefoot and shirtless in the wilds. I spoke with drifters and the homeless, trying to know their hearts and see through their eyes.

Some part of me broke, I think. And then it broke open. That's when I knew what it meant to drink and no longer thirst.

And a strange thing—what had always felt like shattering effort driven by wild thirst suddenly seemed like nothing at all. Perhaps it wasn't my terrible thirst that had driven me all those years. Perhaps I was drawn by the water's thirst for me. And all that strain and adventure, well, that was just the story I told myself along the way.

What has been most odd to me is my return to society since then. I made a conscious choice to rejoin the world, to leave my wild places, to hold a regular job, have a stable home, and reconnect with people. More than a decade later, it still feels strange to me. At times I find myself going through the motions, simply passing as a "normal" person. The challenges of daily life, of paying bills, attending to my body's health, establishing regular patterns others can rely on... these still feel foreign to me, but I consider them a major part of my spiritual practice now. It used to be that the only things that made sense to me were transcendence and escape. These days I find the most humbling truth in being present and watching with wonder, allowing life to simply be as it is.

I'm less consumed by my own thirst these days. I feel the water's thirst for the thirsty world instead.

—〰—

My body is flooded
  With the flame of Love.
  My soul lives in
  A furnace of bliss.

  Love's fragrance
  Fills my mouth,
  And fans through all things
  With each outbreath.

Kabir

English version by Andrew Harvey

My body is flooded ᨆ

This brief, beautiful poem by Kabir feels like it should be repeated during meditation. At first it is a sort of affirmation, then it becomes a map, finally it becomes the experience itself.

> *My body is flooded*
> *With the flame of Love.*

With deep opening, there is a sense of being flooded or even overwhelmed by waves of heat, like flames or a fever. This is felt at both physical and subtle levels. These are the "flames of Love" that flood the body. When we relax into this awareness, the experience is not painful but one of indescribably peaceful delight. This is Kabir's "furnace of bliss."

> *My soul lives in*
> *A furnace of bliss.*

And it is in this furnace, this divine alchemical fire, where the "soul lives." It takes deep stillness and clarity to recognize it, but the soul is always at home within this warm embrace. This is where the soul is seated in perpetual rest, within this sacred, transformative warmth—whether or not we are too distracted to notice.

> *Love's fragrance*
> *Fills my mouth*

Often accompanying the awareness of blissful heat is the sense of a very subtle, wonderfully sweet flavor in the mouth, at the back of the throat. This taste is so subtle that it could be described as a "fragrance," something just barely sensed, yet imprinting itself indelibly upon the awareness.

> *And fans through all things*
> *With each outbreath.*

In this state, when the awareness is turned inward, it is in bliss; when turned outward, there is only the unifying awareness of love. This is what Kabir means when he says, "Love's fragrance... fans through all things / with each outbreath." When we breathe out, when we turn the unified awareness outward, then the perfume of that bliss is carried outward and seen to permeate everything one's perception touches. This leads to a sort of supreme Self-recognition in all things: There is bliss within and bliss without. There is only bliss, and it is flowing everywhere. You yourself are not separate from That. This recognition is the mystic's Love. It is the recognition of unity, the pouring of oneself, one's breath and presence, into all things, with an unhindered and equal flow in return.

Kabir is giving us a map, a grand path of Love that endlessly circles between the inner and outer:

Love
(outer)

fan	flame
flavor	flood

Bliss
(inner)

—⟨⟨⟩⟩—

Love's Living Flame

O love's living flame,
so softly do you sear
the deepest center of my soul!
Now that you no longer shy away,
end this game, I beg of you, today:

Rip open the veil separating us
in this sweet rendezvous!

O tender burn!
O burning boon!
O gentle hand!
O delicate caress,
that infers eternal life
and renders all debts paid!
Killing,
death into life you have made!

O beacons of fire,
in whose splendor
the blind, dark
deep grottoes
of the senses,
with strange and stately art,
warm and enlighten,
and win my love!

How tenderly is your memory
cherished in my breast,
where you alone reside and in secret rest:
Here I taste in your perfumed breath
goodness a-flood with glory—

How gracefully
you've won my love!

John of the Cross

IMG

...A poem to explore the soul's journey of wounding and death, leading to renewed life and openness and integration.

John of the Cross gives us several important themes here worth exploring:

Fire...

In the ecstasy of deep communion, there is often a sense of heat—filled with immense love—that permeates the body. As this fire moves through the body, it also moves through the awareness, consuming all thoughts (or, more accurately, the tremors from which thoughts emerge). This fire burns away even the thought of "I" until only the sense of this living flame remains.

This is such a wonderful fire that mystics often describe it as a flame of love, so enchanting that, like the moth, you want to dart in and be utterly consumed.

This is why John of the Cross refers so passionately to "Love's living flame."

Pain and Wounding...

The notion of wounding as part of the spiritual path has particular significance within mystical Christianity, but we find similar language in all spiritual traditions.

This "pain" has a few levels of meaning. At one level, the pain can be quite literal and even physical. But it might be more accurate to refer to this as intensity rather than pain. It can be as if the senses and the perceptual mind's ability to process it all gets overloaded. The mystic then experiences a searing, cleansing sort of intensity that might be called pain.

Through profound opening, one feels everything more completely, a sort of universal empathy. There is a lot of hidden suffering in the world and, at a certain point, we feel it as our own. (Actually, we always feel it anyway, but in deep communion the walls of denial fall away, and we become aware of it for the first time.) In a   directly   sentient   way,   we   become   aware   of   the interconnectedness of life. Initially, that flood of feeling is intense, even painful, but that is the pain of the heart breaking open. It becomes a sort of wound one carries, but it resolves itself into a beauty and sense of unity that manages to incorporate even the most terrible suffering.

Other mystics speak of a wounding in a more metaphorical sense. The pain experienced is the perception of one's separation from God. But that pain itself is the doorway to reunion. By allowing oneself to become completely vulnerable to that pain, to surrender to it, the mystic finds the pain transformed into the blissful touch of the Beloved.

Ultimately, all of these forms of pain are the pain of the pierced ego. For one with inner balance, where the protective but limiting shell of the ego is no longer necessary, that pain points the way to freedom.

For this reason, mystics and saints describe the pain as being joyful or beautiful. This pain is, in fact, the beginning of bliss.

With all this talk of pain, let's not forget that this pain is not a negative. When we acclimate to the intensity, when the reflex to contain the flood eases, we discover that the overriding sensation is one of sheer bliss.

—⁓⁓—

How is it I can love You
    within me,
      yet see You from afar?

How is it I embrace You
    within myself,
      yet see You spread across the heavens?

You know. You alone.
    You, who made this mystery,
    You who shine
like the sun in my breast,
    You who shine
    in my material heart,
        immaterially.

Symeon the New Theologian

IMG

How is it I can love You ~⌣

The mystic's riddle: How can such immensity be found within? How can the Eternal be discovered within such a limited space as the human awareness? And yet, at the same time, the Eternal permeates the vastness of creation, which itself is ultimately limited. How can this be?

> *How is it I can love You*
> *within me,*
> *yet see You from afar?*

Symeon is not asking these questions as an intellectual game. This is not a dry theological exercise. His questions arise from the genuine surprise at this paradox as it reveals itself through direct perception: The Divine is both intimate and all-encompassing; within, yet everywhere.

> *How is it I embrace You*
> *within myself,*
> *yet see You spread across the heavens?*

In blissful states, we look within and see God. We look outside ourselves, and equally we see God. Near and far: God. Above and below: God. The mountain seats God, but so too does the pebble, and also the mote of dust that settles upon it. Friend—God; enemy—God; self—God.

It cannot be. And yet it is. The intellect balks at it, yet the mystic is confronted with it undeniably. This is not just a pleasant idea; when we really learn to look, this is what we see.

> *You know. You alone.*
> *You, who made this mystery,*
> *You who shine*
> *like the sun in my breast,*
> *You who shine*
> *in my material heart,*
> *immaterially.*

Let theologies try—and fail—to solve this riddle. Let us, instead, join with the world's mystics and watch in wonder.

—〜〜—

Pima Medicine Man's Song

here over you here over you
there is light
it moves about
here over you
there is light
the tassels
downward

Pima Song

English version by George Herzog & Brian Swann

Pima Medicine Man's Song   ～

This medicine song would have been chanted at the completion of a curing ceremony in order to ensure its success.

The light here is the power of spirit, life force, drawn into the body and spirit of the ailing person.

The mention of tassels has a special meaning. For many native peoples of the American Southwest, corn is not only a fundamental food crop, it is central to the sacred imagery, representing the merging of spirit and earth in the form of growing life. Corn is the iconic embodiment of spirit/light/life in the earthly realm. The tassels are specifically corn tassels, and they are pointing downward. One way we can understand the visionary imagery of this medicine song is that the downward pointing corn tassels represent the light of spirit and life flowing downward, streaming directly into the person being healed.

A song affirming healing and life and light...

—⟨∿∿⟩—

I saw a great light come down over London,
And buildings and cars and people were still
They were held wherever they were under the sky's
Clear humming radiance as it descended—
Everywhere, in shops, behind desks and on trains
Everything stopped as the stillness came down
And touched the crown of our heads
As our eyes closed, and the sky filled us
And our minds became the sky—
And everyone, regardless of crime class or creed
Was touched; as slowly we began to stir
Out of this penetrated light-filled sleep
Dizzily as the hand completed its dialing,
And the train lurched forward
And I saw faces looking at one another questioning,
I saw people meeting eye to eye and standing
Half amazed by each other's presence
I saw their mouths silently shaping the word why
Why didn't we know this? and yet knowing
They already knew, and without words
We all stood searching for the gesture
That would say it—

As the lights went green, and we drove on.

Jay Ramsay

I saw a great light   ∿

I saw a great light come down...

That opening phrase, "I saw a great light come down," feels as if it was uttered by Ezekiel or one of the other Old Testament Prophets. But it takes place in present-day London, with buildings and cars and the busy activity of modern city life. That powerful evocation of ancient prophetic vision and modern busyness becomes a brilliant collision that brings us up short and, like the witness of the poem, makes us see things in a new way.

Let me go off on a tangent here for a moment... I was a poor child but raised in an affluent neighborhood in Southern California. Several of my friends lived in large houses with manicured lawns and swimming pools in their back yards. They had two parents, family dinner times, Sunday church or Saturday synagogue. They went on summer vacations.

I had a strange relationship with the world my friends lived in—I wanted its stability, the things and experiences they had, but that normalcy was also alien to me, even a bit eerie. It seemed haunted and unreal. I craved it, but I didn't want to live it.

By the time I was a teenager, I became obsessed with seeing behind the facades of that "normal" reality. I wanted to know what secrets lay hidden in its shadows. I became interested in everything from meditation to history to science to linguistics—all ways to find hidden meaning within the world casually ignored by everyone else.

I also became fascinated by fringe phenomena that upset accepted reality: psychic abilities, cryptozoology... and UFOs. As a teenager I would step outside at night, look up into the infinite void while feeling utterly alien in my own world, and wait for some otherworldly light to come down and bust me free...

Returning to Jay Ramsay's poem, we can read it as a collective moment of awe or of spiritual awakening. But, if we are willing to play loosely with the poet's intentions, we can also read it as a citywide encounter with an unidentified flying object.

It is not entirely clear what is happening in the poem—something spiritual or some unexplained phenomenon of light—just that there is a shared moment of wonder. Everyone stops, confronted with a dazzling new reality. What is actually happening seems less important than the shared nature of the experience. Not only are we witnessing something that transcends the day-to-day, but there is also a connection with everyone else through this magical moment. To me it feels like the reverse of a terrorist event; instead of trauma, everyone comes together in a unifying moment of amazement.

Then, of course, the traffic light turns green, the hovering light moves on or we just stop paying attention, and the business of living continues. But perhaps those people carry just a bit more wonder into their daily activities. And who knows the many subtle, far-reaching ways it will continue to ripple outward through their lives? This is how transformative experiences work their alchemy in the world.

The hunger for meaningful visions and otherworldly encounters, the ache for reality-bending phenomena and celestial escape, they are really our innate yearning for wonder. The irony is that wonder is right here in us waiting for us to stop and notice the mystery already hovering in our midst.

—⁓—

The Light of Your Way

You have flooded my heart
   with the light of your way,

and you have raised up in me
   the Tree of Life.

You have shown me a new heaven
   upon the earth.
You have shown me a secret Garden,
   unseen within the seen.

Now am I joined soul and spirit
   present in your Presence—

your Presence that has waited long in me,
your Presence, the true Tree of Life,
   planted in whatever this earth is,
   planted in whatever it is that men are,
      planted, and rooted in the heart,

your Presence all at once revealing your Paradise
alive with every good green thing:
   grasses and trees and the fruiting bounty,
   a world of flowers!
      sweet-scented lilies!

Each little flower speaks a truth:
   humility and joy,
   peace, oh peace!
   kindness, compassion,
      the turning of the soul,

and the flood of tears
and the strange ecstasy
of those bathed in your light.

Symeon the New Theologian

IMG

The Light of Your Way ~

Notice the imagery of light (a constant theme in Symeon's poetry)—

> *for you have flooded my heart*
> *with the light of your way...*

—and the Tree of Life—

> *and you have raised up in me*
> *the Tree of Life.*

These lead us to recognize God's Presence within:

> *Now am I joined soul and spirit*
> *present in your Presence—*

> *your Presence that has waited long in me...*

Knowing the sacred Presence, our blindness is removed and we finally see through the surface of things.

> *You have shown me a new heaven*
> *upon the earth.*
> *You have shown me a secret Garden,*
> *unseen within the seen.*

We discover the heaven that has always been hidden within the earth, shining beneath the gauze of the seen.

That leads to a startling realization: All of creation, the living earth itself, is a sacred, living garden, waiting for our eyes to open.

> *your Presence all at once revealing your Paradise*
> *alive with every good green thing:*
> > *grasses and trees and the fruiting bounty,*
> > *a world of flowers!*
> > > *sweet-scented lilies!*

People are always looking for their paradise somewhere else, somewhere outside their lives, when it is always and ever right

118

here, within, inside this very present moment, present in the Presence. The problem is in how we see the living planet and our own selves—or, rather, how we don't see them.

> *your Presence, the true Tree of Life,*
> > *planted in whatever this earth is,*
> > *planted in whatever it is that men are,*
> > > *planted, and rooted in the heart...*

The Tree of Life is the center of the Garden, yet it is rooted in the heart. When we finally see it within, we see it everywhere, for it fills our awareness. As we find our hearts and discover the real life within, we naturally interact with each other and the planet in awe and reverence.

In this way we steadily reveal paradise to one another.

> *Each little flower speaks a truth:*
> > *humility and joy,*
> > *peace, oh peace!*
> > *kindness, compassion,*
> > > *the turning of the soul,*
>
> > *and the flood of tears*
> > *and the strange ecstasy*
> > > *of those bathed in your light.*

—⌇∿⌇—

Reason

Let reason go. For His light
burns reason up from head to foot.

If you wish to see that Face,
seek another eye. The philosopher
with his two eyes sees double,
so is unable to see the unity of the Truth.

As His light burns up the angels,
even so does it consume reason.
As the light of our eyes is to the sun,
so is the light of reason to the Light of Lights.

Shabistari

English version by Florence Lederer

Reason ∿

Shabistari is telling us some surprising things in these verses, evoking words of light, sight, reason, and truth.

We can't see "the Face" (of God) with the eyes of reason. The philosopher who seeks to understand the nature of reality with reason "sees double" with "two eyes." The logical mind is dualistic. It cannot see beyond the multiplicity of material existence. Even in its most elevated theorizing, it is still limited by its concepts, which are, by definition, segmented parcels of reality. The Face, however, is the wholeness of that reality, and beyond the reasoning mind's grasp.

Reason is a powerful tool, but it only sees certain things and from a certain perspective. To see the Face, we must go beyond the double vision of reason and "seek another eye." We must discover the eye that is single, one that is able "to see the unity of the Truth."

Shabistari keeps returning us to a vision of light that burns away everything. It "burns reason up from head to foot." It even "burns up the angels." What is this "Light of Lights" that consumes everything within itself?

Light is often used in sacred language and poetry to suggest intelligence, awareness, consciousness. There is a "light of reason," but its radiance is faint compared to the "Light of Lights." For genuine mystics, this light is not a mere concept; it is directly experienced.

The mystic's light, when finally witnessed, is more than the brightness one might experience on a sunny afternoon. This light is perceived as a living radiance that permeates everything, everywhere, always. This light is immediately understood to be the true source of all things, the foundation on which the physicality of the material world is built.

The sense of boundaries and separation, long taken for granted by the mind as the fundamental nature of existence, suddenly seems illusory, for this light shines through all people and things. It has no edges, and the light of one is the light of another. Everything "burns up" in the light.

121

This light is the vision of the "unity of Truth." It is "that Face." Beyond limited concepts, the mind can only stop and stare in wonder, its reason burned "from head to foot."

—⁓—

I lost my world, my fame, my mind—
The Sun appeared, and all the shadows ran.
I ran after them, but vanished as I ran—
Light ran after me and hunted me down.

Rumí

English version by Andrew Harvey

I lost my world, my fame, my mind ∽

The Sun appeared, and all the shadows ran.

Many of Rumi's poems summon images of the sun. This has layered meaning for Rumi since he was deeply devoted to his spiritual teacher, Shams of Tabriz... The name Shams means "the sun."

The sun for Rumi can be God, or the radiance of God shining through his beloved teacher, or the light of enlightenment. Though why should we separate them out? They are all the same Divine continuum.

The light of God comes, enlightenment shines, and shadows disappear.

In that light, we see things simply and purely as they are, not as we are told they are. Standing outside the shadow world of mundane reality, we realize that the roles we play in life have not come with us into that brilliant stillness. The mind and all its clamoring thoughts have also been left behind—

I lost my world, my fame, my mind—

Filled with that light, surrounded by the light, all of existence inter-permeated by that light, we can search for some root or tendril of those things that once seemed so immutable and defining, but the more we search, the more we recognize how gossamer thin the very fabric of our own identity actually is.

I ran after them, but vanished as I ran—
Light ran after me and hunted me down.

Then it hits us: We are not really "selves," we are not the distinct nuggets of identity commonly imagined. We are not even illumined beings surrounded and permeated by light. There is only light, and no "I" in the midst of it. The only "self" we can claim is not really a separate being but, rather, a distinct point-of-view within one immense, shining Being. The enlightened mystic sees only that light, dancing and playing, sometimes eddying into "me" and "you" and all the world, without actually losing its luminescent nature or flow.

125

So, seekers, while you are on your spiritual hunt, remember to look over your shoulder. The glow you glimpse might just be hunting you.

—*∿∿*—

On Those Words "I am for My Beloved"

Already I gave myself completely,
and have changed in such a way
That my Beloved is for me
and I am for my Beloved.

When the gentle hunter shot me
and left me in all my weakness,
in the arms of love
my soul fell
and being charged with new life
I have changed in such a way
That My Beloved is for me
and I am for my Beloved.

He pierced me with an arrow
laced with the herbs of love
and my soul became one
with her Creator;
I no longer want another love,
since I have given myself to my God,
That My Beloved is for me
and I am for my Beloved.

Teresa of Avila

English version by Megan Don

On Those Words "I am for My Beloved"   ∾

This poem by Teresa of Avila was written about a mystical experience she had, in which she felt her heart pierced with divine love by an angel. That well-known sacred encounter also inspired Bernini to sculpt his masterpiece of the enraptured Teresa.

A few of my own thoughts:

Saints and mystics the world over speak of the heart being touched, pierced, opened. They speak of an overwhelming encounter with love. The problem is, we hear the words "love" and "heart" and we think of the simple sweetness of Valentine's Day cards. We aren't encouraged to develop a real concept of what these great souls are attempting to communicate.

When the mind settles and the soul waits in courageously vulnerable readiness, the most amazing thing happens: the heart blooms. The heart opens and expands. Effortlessly, the heart reaches out, with a wider span than we ever imagined possible, embracing all of creation. We become flooded with something beyond feeling or emotion. There is a sense of finally recognizing one's very nature within the heart, that this is the seat of our being.

When focused inward, we are enraptured, filled with bliss. When focused outward, we are an embodiment of love. We begin to feel so much more, all the world's suffering and searching and occasional surges of life, and it is all beautiful and somehow a part of us.

Think about these things. Consider what it means to have the heart truly "pierced" by the Divine. How do we prepare ourselves? How can we, in full honesty, say, "I gave myself completely," and "I am for my Beloved"? What is the weakness or vulnerability that the "gentle hunter" leaves us in? What does it mean to be "changed with new life"? And the big question: What is the real experience that allows us to say, "my soul became one / with her Creator"?

—✎✎✎—

Love

O nectar! O delicious stream!
O ravishing and only pleasure! Where
    Shall such another theme
Inspire my tongue with joys or please mine ear!
    Abridgement of delights!
    And Queen of sights!
O mine of rarities! O Kingdom wide!
O more! O cause of all! O glorious Bride!
    O God! O Bride of God! O King!
    O soul and crown of everything!

    Did not I covet to behold
Some endless monarch, that did always live
    In palaces of gold,
Willing all kingdoms, realms, and crowns to give
    Unto my soul! Whose love
    A spring might prove
Of endless glories, honours, friendships, pleasures,
Joys, praises, beauties and celestial treasures!
    Lo, now I see there's such a King.
    The fountain-head of everything!

    Did my ambition ever dream
Of such a Lord, of such a love! Did I
    Expect so sweet a stream
As this at any time! Could any eye
    Believe it? Why all power
    Is used here;
Joys down from Heaven on my head do shower,
And Jove beyond the fiction doth appear
    Once more in golden rain to come
    To Danae's pleasing fruitful womb.

His Ganymede! His life! His joy!
Or He comes down to me, or takes me up
    That I might be His boy,
And fill, and taste, and give, and drink the cup.
    But those (tho' great) are all
    Too short and small,
Too weak and feeble pictures to express
The true mysterious depths of Blessedness.
    I am His image, and His friend,
    His son, bride, glory, temple, end.

Thomas Traherne

Love ∾

This poem by Traherne is almost breathless in its ecstatic exclamations. Though highly structured in meter and rhyme, he just barely seems to be able to get the words onto the page.

The first verse is an overwhelm of bliss and images: nectar, a stream, a kingdom, a king, a bride, a crown.

Why does Traherne start his poem with descriptions of "nectar," a "delicious steam" that more than anything else can "inspire my tongue with joys"? The ecstatic state is often interpreted by the sense-mind as a beautiful, rich sweetness on the upper palette and at the back of the throat, accompanied by warmth in the belly. There is also a visual awareness of a glowing gold or white color coming down from above ("golden rain"). One may feel a blissful giddiness and, sometimes, a trembling that can mimic drunkenness, so mystics also refer to this subtle liquid as wine: "And fill, and taste, and give, and drink the cup."

In Christian symbolic language, the King, of course, is Christ, or more generally the personal aspect of God. The Bride is the purified individual soul that joins with the Divine and discovers ecstasy in holy union.

In the second verse, Traherne lists what he had been seeking all his life, that which he imagined God to be: endless power, love, glory, beauty, the source of everything. But the next verse moves out of the conceptual to a revelation of what he has actually witnessed. And he is flabbergasted to discover that as rich as his mental concepts of the Divine had been, the direct experience is greater still:

> *Did my ambition ever dream*
> *Of such a Lord, of such love!*

Love, true divine love that rejects nothing and embraces everything, is just a philosophical idea until it is actually felt— and then you realize the idea hardly hinted at the reality. This is accompanied by a sense of wholeness and of bliss that descends upon the awareness:

> *Joys down from Heaven on my head do shower.*

132

The final section is the most personal.

> *Once more in golden rain to come*
> *To Danae's pleasing fruitful womb.*

> *His Ganymede! His life! His joy!*

Traherne sees himself as Danae embraced by the divine golden shower of Ganymede, the cupbearer of heaven. The divine living source of everything has, in the most intimate way, touched and claimed him.

> *But those (tho' great) are all*
> *Too short and small,*
> *Too weak and feeble pictures to express*
> *The true mysterious depths of Blessedness.*

But even these descriptions "tho' great" can't do justice to the reality. There are no satisfactory words for "The true mysterious depths of Blessedness." The best he can do to put this relationship into words is to view it as encompassing all relationships—friend, son, bride—and to recognize himself as a reflection of the Divine, an intimate, a vessel, a completed work—image, glory, temple, end:

> *I am His image, and His friend,*
> *His son, bride, glory, temple, end.*

—⁓—

Waiting

The jeweled cloud sways overhead,
waiting.
Meanwhile, our cells are turning to air,
finer and finer arrangements of light.

Dorothy Walters

In these few lines, Dorothy Walters suggests that spiritual transformation is also physical transformation down to the cellular level. Our bodies become "finer and finer arrangements of light." What a great line! I imagine the body as a shimmering web of filaments and cells, somehow elevated, made lighter, subtler, and vivified by the infusion of new awareness so the body's network reorganizes itself into ever more artistic patterns of itself.

We find intimations of this idea in various sacred traditions. The body of light. The body of bliss. A new body in Christ. The Kabbalist's Merkava. The perfected body in alchemy. The shaman's body. The adamantine body in Yoga and Buddhism. The Taoist's immortal body.

What most mystics speak of when using these terms is that the body has been recollected into the full awareness: It is whole and complete. The body knows itself and knows it is alive. It finally feels the stream of life running through it. Most importantly, the body becomes a vehicle capable of participating in the greater wholeness of divine union.

> *Meanwhile, our cells are turning to air,*
> *finer and finer arrangements of light.*

IV
Only the Mountain Remains

Mountains
mirrored in his eye—
dragonfly.

Issa

IMG

Mountains 〜

Imagine a dragonfly. It is beautiful, ephemeral, ethereal. Its wings are translucent, yet glisten with rainbow colors when they catch the light. On summer days the dragonfly darts about, almost impossible to catch, then hovers in midair, contemplating the world about it.

And its eyes, in Issa's haiku, reflect.

One way to understand this poem is that the dragonfly represents the mind that has become self-aware, resplendent and delighting in its intangible beauty. It darts here and there and then stabilizes. In recognizing its own insignificance, it becomes alive to the immense world of wonder that surrounds it.

In this way, even a dragonfly's minute eye reflects the grandeur of mountains. The mind, in its stillness, manages to reflect the immensity of eternity.

—〰—

The Absolute works with nothing.
The workshop, the materials
are what does not exist.

Try and be a sheet of paper with nothing on it.
Be a spot of ground where nothing is growing,
where something might be planted,
a seed, possibly, from the Absolute.

Rumí

English version by Coleman Barks

The Absolute works with nothing   ∾

This one got me thinking...

We are always making plans, building ourselves up, and projecting ourselves into the world. Amidst this constant fullness, Rumi reminds us that we must also have emptiness. If our hands are not empty, they cannot receive. For the soil to be ready for the seed, it must first be cleared.

Empty receptivity, that takes real courage. It requires the courage to be at ease with blank, still spaces in the soul, the courage to feel our own fecundity hidden beneath all our activity. Instead of filling that emptiness, we learn to wait, trusting that some new spark will land and glow and grow.

—◊◊◊—

God, whose love and joy are present everywhere,
  Can't come to visit you unless you aren't there.

Angelus Silesius

English version by Gabriel Rosenstock

God, whose love and joy ~

This *koan*-like couplet by Angelus Silesius has two statements of God's presence that cause the logical mind to somersault. First, God "can't come to visit you unless you aren't there." And, second, we have to ask, how God "whose love and joy are present everywhere," can "visit" anywhere since a visit implies that God isn't already there?

Think for a moment what Angelus Silesius is saying in these few words. God "can't come to visit" unless "you," the ego-self, is no longer present. The ego identity, though normally assumed to be one's entire self, can, through spiritual practice and deep surrender, fall away. When there is no longer any "you" there, the radiant, loving, blissful presence of the Divine is perceived everywhere, even where "you" once were. This is when God has "come to visit you"... but it won't happen "unless you aren't there"!

—⁓⁓—

Sitting (Reverence Mountain)

A flock of birds flies up, then disappears.
One last cloud also drifts into emptiness.

The mountain and I gaze at each other,
Untiring, until only the mountain remains.

Li Bai

English version by Doug Westendorp

Sitting (Reverence Mountain) ∼

This poem describes a perfect quiet moment in nature, and that may be enough. Yet, we can also see in this poem a precise meditation on mind witnessing the *Tao*.

One way to read Li Bai's poem is that the birds are like chattering thoughts. They represent movement within the mind. But thoughts can soar to such heights that they vanish in the mind's sky-like emptiness.

The last cloud might be understood as the last clinging disruptions of awareness, obscuring perception of the vast sky-mind. Along with the birds, the cloud, too, "drifts into emptiness."

The mountain is that which is eternal, fixed, rooted in the earth while touching the heavens. Watching this mountain long enough, stillness settles upon us and we discover that whatever "I" may be is nowhere to be seen—"only the mountain remains." The mountain is finally recognized as our true self, the only Self, that which is eternal. Effortlessly, we bridge heaven and earth by our very nature. And only That remains.

Or—

You can ignore all of that, and just step into the landscape.

—∿∿—

An Exquisite Truth

This is an exquisite truth:
Saints and ordinary folks are the same from the start.
Inquiring about a difference
Is like asking to borrow string
When you've got a good strong rope.
Every Dharma is known in the heart.
After a rain, the mountain colors intensify.
Once you become familiar with the design of fate's illusions
Your ink-well will contain all of life and death.

Hsu Yun

English version by The Zen Buddhist Order of Hsu Yun

An Exquisite Truth ~⌣

I like what that opening statement says:

> *This is an exquisite truth:*
> *Saints and ordinary folks are the same from the start.*

Whether we're talking about inspired reformers or shining examples of enlightenment, our instinct is to elevate great souls as unique phenomena. We assume they are somehow other than us. But the liberating and challenging truth is that saints are the same as everyone else. The only difference, if we want to call it a difference, is that they don't cloak their nature as most of us have learned to do. We all have that same steady glow within us. A saint is simply someone who doesn't damp it down.

Understood this way, the spiritual journey is not one of crushing effort to acquire virtues, to build wisdom, and to learn love. We already have all of that in abundance. The only work necessary is to let go of the assumptions that keep our true nature hidden.

> *Once you become familiar with the design of fate's*
> *illusions*
> *Your ink-well will contain all of life and death.*

I think these are the lines I respond to most. I don't know about you, but I spent so much of my life as a teenager and young adult feeling disappointed with where I found myself in the world. I wanted something profound, adventurous, bursting with meaning. Instead, I had a very ordinary lower middle-class American upbringing. I sabotaged my college education and decided to search for something deeper. Most of that search was a painful flailing about, but it did bring me adventures, both internal and external. I lived on Maui for several years. I lived high up in the Rocky Mountains. I've been homeless. I've had friends in wheelchairs, friends with wealth. I've known hippies and bikers and techies and farmers.

While all of that makes for good stories, that ache for something extraordinary just fell away the moment I first settled into a sense of spiritual opening. With that dawning of peace, I also found rest... and a profound sense of self-acceptance. It wasn't that I had somehow changed into someone new and

147

extraordinary. Instead, I felt profoundly myself for the first time, profoundly my ordinary self. And I can't describe how blissful that recognition of ordinariness is. I no longer felt the constant need to struggle after the extraordinary; the simple and the plain stood revealed as a stunning work of art filling every day.

These lines by Hsu Yun about "fate's illusions" remind me of how I spent the first three decades of my life struggling against my circumstances to find a fate with meaning, only to discover that the struggle was unnecessary. All I had to do was open my eyes. In every corner of the world, in every life, great and humble, the entire mystery of life and death can be found.

After a rain, the mountain colors intensify.

———∿∿∿———

Love came and emptied me of self,
every vein and every pore,
made into a container to be filled by the Beloved.
Of me, only a name is left,
the rest is You my Friend, my Beloved.

Abu-Said Abil-Kheir

English version by Vraje Abramian

Love came and emptied me of self ∼ᵒ

I have dealt with chronic fatigue on and off for years. As part of that pattern, I sometimes feel an intense sensation of tremors, even though my body is entirely still. Sitting on the couch with my wife, I'll turn to see if she is shaking her foot, causing the couch to vibrate. But, no, she is quietly sitting there with no agitating movements. Each time this happens I'm surprised to find that nothing is actually shaking at all, neither my body nor the environment around me.

When the chronic fatigue symptoms are that strong I usually don't have the energy to do a full day's work, yet my body isn't at rest enough to meditate either. What is a person to do who strives to be "spiritual," when he can neither meditate nor take action? Interesting things happen at such moments.

When the stories we tell ourselves about ourselves can no long be sustained, one option is to cling to the crumbling edifice and be injured by its collapse. Another option is to construct a new story. Or we can let all stories fall away. We can stop struggling to be either this or that. We can step beyond our stories. That is when we rediscover what we actually are. That is when hidden doorways open.

The little self is simply the sum total of all the stories we tell ourselves. When those stories fall away, the self becomes empty of itself. We then become a cup, empty and ready to be filled.

> *Of me, only a name is left,*
> *the rest is You my Friend, my Beloved.*

This is the hard wisdom that chronic illness teaches. Any life struggle—really any experience, pleasant or unpleasant—can be transformed into a teacher of wisdom when we stop taking it personally. Wisdom roots itself most deeply when we keep our hearts engaged and our eyes open in the midst of our shifting self-stories.

What can one do but stand in silent awe of the vision that emerges, showing us how much bigger we are than even our grandest stories?

—◦◦◦—

151

"I" and "You"

"I" and "you" are but the lattices
In the niches of a lamp,
Through which the One Light shines.

"I" and "you" are the veil
Between heaven and earth;
Lift this veil and you will see
No longer the bond of sects and creeds.

When "I" and "you" do not exist,
What is mosque, what is synagogue?
What is the Temple of Fire?

Shabistari

English version by Florence Lederer

"I" and "You"—What is Shabistari talking about here? "I" and "You" is the normal perception of existence. Here "I" stand, and "You" are a separate entity over there. It is the perception of duality in which we see the entire universe as a fragmented space of disconnected beings and objects. On the one hand, that perception allows us to feel supremely important in contrast to all else, but it also isolates us and imprisons us in a physicalized notion of reality. Even when we touch, we never quite make contact. The heart ever yearns for real unity.

To show us the way out of this perceptual trap, Shabistari has given us an image to contemplate: a lamp surrounded by latticework. The lamp shines with a single light, but the lattices divide up the radiance into several individual shafts of light. He tells us the world of separation between "I" and "You" is like that—one light divided into many rays.

Think about this image for a moment. So long as we look outward, we only see separated beams of light reaching through the air and patterning the wall. But the moment it occurs to us to look at the lamp itself, we turn around and discover the single light that is its source within. Finally seeing that one light, we then know that there has only ever been that one light. Does the lattice somehow create many lights of the one light? No. It is still the one light, but expressing itself through the many beams. To prove this to ourselves, all we need do is remove the latticework, and then the light shines everywhere, undivided. And the whole time the light itself has never changed its action or nature.

Shabistari makes an interesting shift in the second part of this verse. The separation of "I" and "You" expands to encompass the realm of the world's religious divisions. And the metaphor of the lamp's lattice has become a veil (which, of course, covers the face of the Beloved). Even the many sects and religions are one—when we finally look inward toward the light that shines at the heart of each tradition. To one who has lifted the veil and witnessed the underlying Beauty, the distinctions of each tradition and theology no longer separate them. Instead, we can say that the best of each religious tradition adorns the Face differently—but it is the same Face.

Lift this veil...

...and separation is lost, the soul's isolation ends. And every place becomes a place of worship.

—✦—

Liberation From All Obstructions

"In the presence of Sangha, in the light of Dharma,
in oneness with Buddha—may my path
to complete enlightenment benefit everyone!"

In this passing moment karma ripens
and all things come to be.
I vow to choose what is:
If there is cost, I choose to pay.
If there is need, I choose to give.
If there is pain, I choose to feel.
If there is sorrow, I choose to grieve.
When burning—I choose heat.
When calm—I choose peace.
When starving—I choose hunger.
When happy—I choose joy.
Whom I encounter, I choose to meet.
What I shoulder, I choose to bear.
When it is my death, I choose to die.
Where this takes me, I choose to go.
Being with what is—I respond to what is.

This life is as real as a dream;
the one who knows it cannot be found;
and, truth is not a thing—Therefore I vow
to choose THIS dharma entrance gate!
May all Buddhas and Wise Ones
help me live this vow.

Hogan Bays

Liberation From All Obstructions ∿

There's something both delightful and deeply challenging about this vow poem.

The entire poem is summed up at the beginning:

I vow to choose what is

You would think the unavoidable nature of "what is" makes a statement like this meaningless, but the human mind is not entirely sane. It often chooses fantasy and imaginings, shoulds and coulds, possibilities and even impossibilities over what *is*. Very few of us truly dwell in reality. Rarely do we fully experience the moments of our lives.

What is it that we are straining for as we constantly lean away from "what is"? What do we think is missing that we need? We don't need someone else's life. We don't need a perfect marriage, better finances, or a better place in society. We don't even need to be a saint living in the mountains. What's missing is ourselves. What we really need is to stand in our own shoes, to be utterly ourselves. We need that missing ingredient—being present. We need to live, with honesty and an open heart, the life that already moves through us.

When starving—I choose hunger.
When happy—I choose joy.

When we are hungry, can we choose anything other than hunger? When happy, isn't joy automatic? The truth is that we constantly choose. Ask yourself, how often do we really sit with our hunger and sorrow? How often do we allow ourselves to dance with the joy bubbling up inside us? How often do we notice these things at all?

The power of a practice like Zen is that it defines the human journey, not as escape, but as coming home, of settling into ourselves and being present with the present. It challenges us to actually live the moment that continuously arrives and passes and renews itself.

By making this journey to "what is," we finally meet ourselves and learn what this amazing thing is that we call life, with all its rich, joyful, painful, and transitory beauty.

May all Buddhas and Wise Ones
help me live this vow.

———∿∿∿———

You are Christ's Hands

Christ has no body now on earth but yours,
     no hands but yours,
     no feet but yours,
Yours are the eyes through which is to look out
     Christ's compassion to the world
Yours are the feet with which he is to go about
     doing good;
Yours are the hands with which he is to bless men now.

Teresa of Avila (attributed)

You are Christ's Hands ~

This is a prayer of supreme spiritual maturity. It is not someone imploring Christ to come and fix everything; rather, it recognizes the presence of the Divine within each of us, and acknowledges our sacred responsibility to embody that compassion and service to the world. Each one of us is the vehicle through which Christ (or *Ishwara* or the Buddha) enacts blessings in the world. Our job is to get out of the way and let that sacred current flow through us unhindered.

Yours are the hands with which he is to bless men now...

—⁓—

V

Beyond Knowing

In the market, in the cloister—only God I saw.
In the valley and on the mountain—only God I saw.
Him I have seen beside me oft in tribulation;
In favour and in fortune—only God I saw.
In prayer and fasting, in praise and contemplation,
In the religion of the Prophet—only God I saw.
Neither soul nor body, accident nor substance,
Qualities nor causes—only God I saw.
I opened mine eyes and by the light of His face around me
In all the eye discovered—only God I saw.
Like a candle I was melting in His fire:
Amidst the flames outflashing—only God I saw.
Myself with mine own eyes I saw most clearly,
But when I looked with God's eyes—only God I saw.
I passed away into nothingness, I vanished,
And lo, I was the All-living—only God I saw.

Baba Kuhi of Shiraz

English version by Reynold A. Nicholson

Only God I saw ∼ෟ

We have a tendency to read a poem like this with its repeated statement—"only God I saw"—as a sort of affirmation, as if the poet is coaxing the awareness, convincing it to see only God everywhere. Those who are inspired by this see it as an image of training the awareness to perceive a wider, interconnected reality; while others may reject it as a sort of willing self-delusion or self-hypnosis. Both of these perspectives assume effort in the seeing.

But perhaps neither is correct. Yes, it's true that in the path of seeking truth, there is necessary effort in seeing, and learning how to see. But there is a certain threshold that is passed where an entirely different form of perception occurs, where one simply sees things as they are. With no effort. No will. No self. Nothing left to cloud the inner eye. That is when seeing finally occurs for the first time.

And what does one see? A radiant, living reality in which all things flow one into the other. Or perhaps you might just say, "Only God I saw."

Still there are forms about you, mountains and valleys, people and their busy world—but all of that seems like a shifting glaze upon the surface of the shining reality. Nothing has any real or tangible substance in and of itself. Even your own body, even your own sense of individuality, are seen as phantom-like, the very idea of them disappearing into that living radiance.

No matter where you look, you find yourself proclaiming—"only God I saw."

See for yourself.

—⸺⸺—

The Further You Go

Mercy, there have been revelations.
Grace, there has been realisation. Still, you must
travel the path of time and circumstance.

The further you go, the more it comes back to paying
    attention.
The rough skin of the tallowwood, the trade routes of
    lorikeets, a sky lifting
behind afternoon clouds. Staying close to the texture of
    things.

People can go before you and talk all they want,
but only one thing makes sense: the way the world enters
and finds its voice in you: the place you are free.

Andrew Colliver

> *Mercy, there have been revelations.*
> *Grace, there has been realisation. Still, you must*
> *travel the path of time and circumstance.*

Those opening lines say something that isn't said often enough: Even with that sweet touch of mercy and grace, amidst the flood of bliss and enlightenment's dawning, "Still, you must travel the path of time and circumstance."

After being enrapt by such full, spacious silence, we are disoriented by the recognition that rent is still due, dishes still wait to be done. I think we so romanticize states of opening that we imagine all work and responsibility will evaporate. Yet the world goes on and, if we are not living in a forest or a cave, we must still answer its demands.

So then we start asking ourselves just what this revelation or realization actually means.

> *The further you go, the more it comes back to paying*
> *attention.*

This poem suggests to me that our opening becomes its own practice. We discover a new sense of self that encounters the world more fully, with more fully engaged awareness, allowing something big to express itself through us in our simple daily activities.

In the collapse of our fantasies of enlightenment, we discover the opportunity to live an embodied enlightenment, instead. The result may not look much like enlightenment at all. No robes, no blissfully glassy gaze, no gathering of disciples, just an ordinary person leading an ordinary life. Except that that ordinary life starts to ring with a certain quiet resonance. It touches and transforms. It sees the secret glistening beneath the world's hard surfaces. It speaks with a new and truer voice.

> *but only one thing makes sense: the way the world enters*
> *and finds its voice in you: the place you are free.*

167

The Night

Through that pure Virgin-shrine,
That sacred veil drawn o'er thy glorious noon
That men might look and live as glow-worms shine,
And face the moon:
Wise Nicodemus saw such light
As made him know his God by night.

Most blest believer he!
Who in that land of darkness and blind eyes
Thy long expected healing wings could see,
When thou didst rise,
And what can never more be done,
Did at mid-night speak with the Sun!

O who will tell me, where
He found thee at that dead and silent hour!
What hallowed solitary ground did bear
So rare a flower,
Within whose sacred leaves did lie
The fullness of the Deity.

No mercy-seat of gold,
No dead and dusty Cherub, nor carved stone,
But his own living works did my Lord hold
And lodge alone;
Where trees and herbs did watch and peep
And wonder, while the Jews did sleep.

Dear night! this world's defeat;
The stop to busy fools; care's check and curb;
The day of Spirits; my soul's calm retreat
Which none disturb!
Christ's progress, and his prayer time;
The hours to which high Heaven doth chime.

God's silent, searching flight:
When my Lord's head is filled with dew, and all
His locks are wet with the clear drops of night;
        His still, soft call;
    His knocking time; the soul's dumb watch,
    When Spirits their fair kindred catch.

        Were all my loud, evil days
Calm and unhaunted as is thy dark Tent,
Whose peace but by some Angel's wing or voice
        Is seldom rent;
    Then I in Heaven all the long year
    Would keep, and never wander here.

        But living where the sun
Doth all things wake, and where all mix and tire
Themselves and others, I consent and run
        To every mire,
    And by this world's ill-guiding light,
    Err more than I can do by night.

        There is in God (some say)
A deep, but dazzling darkness; as men here
Say it is late and dusky, because they
        See not all clear;
    O for that night! where I in him
    Might live invisible and dim.

Henry Vaughan

The Night ∽

Let me first point out that this is a poem to be read out loud. Actually, all poems, except perhaps for some post-modern poems, are intended to be read aloud. Always remember, poetry is not about quietly reading from a book. Poetry requires us to make some noise!

If you just look at Henry Vaughan's lines on the page, your eyes will tend to skim through the words and not really take them in. This is a poem with rhyme and meter—and life!—but all of that is easy to miss, unless you read it aloud.

So go ahead, turn some heads, read out loud, feel this poem on your tongue. Several of the lines are worth savoring... tasty poetry!

Henry Vaughan starts off by recalling the Christian gospel story of Nicodemus visiting Christ in secret at night. He plays with the English pun of Christ as both Sun and Son. Thus, Nicodemus accomplishes a most amazing feat when he "Did at mid-night speak with the Sun!"

More broadly, this poem is a meditation on night as the initiator of light. It is when the worldly sphere is in darkness, when its endless activity comes to rest ("the stop to busy fools") that the mind settles and we have the opportunity to turn inward. It is in the womb of night that we stop our constant distractions. Then the light of spiritual awakening can be perceived.

But there is an even deeper meaning here, one that is more consciously mystical.

> *There is in God (some say)*
> *A deep, but dazzling darkness...*

That reference to "dazzling darkness" directly quotes a phrase from the hugely influential Christian mystical writings of Dionysius (who probably lived around 500 AD). Dionysius wrote that the "immutable mysteries of divine truth are hidden in the *dazzling darkness* of inner silence, outshining all light with the intensity of their darkness."

This "dazzling darkness" is a way to describe the state of awareness experienced in deep communion. Normally, we don't see reality directly; we see, instead, our mental projections draped over reality. When the mind settles into stillness, that self-generated layer on top of reality fades out of sight, and the reality we witness is no longer the same. The act of seeing itself has radically changed into something entirely new.

We can say that seeing (in the normal sense) stops, but perception opens. A person is no longer seen as a person, a table is no longer a table. Surfaces and categories—the foundation of mundane perception—become ephemeral, dreamlike, insubstantial. We no longer see the hard crust of reality, and this can be compared to blindness or darkness. The firm details of surface-level reality fade into the background of perception, as if one's sight has been lost, while the underlying glow fills the awareness. In this "darkness" everything shines!

This is the dazzling darkness. This is why many mystics assert they no longer see the world and, instead, see only God. It is not that they start bumping into furniture when they walk across a room. Perception on the mundane level doesn't stop (except in the most ecstatic states), but surfaces take on a thin or unreal quality; it only occupies a minimal level of the awareness. This is the way you can "at mid-night speak with the Sun!"

—∿∿—

Millennium Blessing

There is a grace approaching
that we shun as much as death,
it is the completion of our birth.

It does not come in time,
        but in timelessness
when the mind sinks into the heart
and we remember.

It is an insistent grace that draws us
to the edge and beckons us to surrender
safe territory and enter our enormity.

We know we must pass
        beyond knowing
and fear the shedding.

But we are pulled upward
        none-the-less
through forgotten ghosts
        and unexpected angels,
luminous.

And there is nothing left to say
but we are That.

And that is what we sing about.

Stephen Levine

Millennium Blessing   ∿

That opening statement is so true—

> *There is a grace approaching*
> *that we shun as much as death,*
> *it is the completion of our birth.*

Most of us spend our entire lives avoiding that inner opening. It is that quiet itch at the back of the awareness that makes us squirm and turn away. And when it really presses on us, it can arouse terror, as if we were facing down death.

That's the thing: That oh-so-sweet moment of awakening is only sweet on the other side of the threshold. But to approach it *is* to face death. It is the death of our old worldview, the death of patterned awareness, the death of our limited notion of who we are. All we thought ourselves to be stops—and so it *is* a sort of death. To feel that grace approaching, to welcome it, requires a wild sort of courage.

> *It is an insistent grace that draws us*
> *to the edge and beckons us to surrender*
> *safe territory and enter our enormity.*

It requires courage and, yes, surrender. We have this idea that spiritual opening is a terrible effort. No. That unfolding *wants* to occur within us. The only effort is to let go of our endless strategies to halt the process. We all feel it, a gentle prodding to let the heart open, to know ourselves truly, to be present and radiate ourselves into the world.

That opening is insistent, trying to happen within us. Call it grace, if you like. The question is before us: Do we courageously accept the invitation to grace?

> *It does not come in time,*
> > *but in timelessness*
> *when the mind sinks into the heart*
> *and we remember.*

For those of us who live in modern urban society, think how hard it is to stop the ticking of the clock. From an early age we internalize the sense of time and progress and deadlines. Yet, in doing so, we forget that these are all just concepts, just one way to understand the unfolding of being and experience. That sense of time is a powerful tool for doing and accomplishment, but it isn't inherently real. It doesn't have much to do with who or what we are. There is a flow of days and months, but they are the surface current of a much deeper timelessness.

I remember as a young man trying to figure out what timelessness was. I sought to live in remote places. I got rid of the television (to which, as a child raised on 70s sitcoms, I had a serious addiction). I spent a lot of time in nature. I slowly learned to let go of the endless buzzing of thoughts. This might sound like a brutal endurance sport, but that wasn't how I experienced it. I wanted to feel what life was without the filters of the 20th century mindset and 20th century time. I wanted to know who I was in the space of timelessness.

It is fascinating how we use the hyperactivity of thought to define the world, to frame our perception of the world, and in some ways to limit our notion of the world. The other thing about thought: It creates time. When thought settles down, we discover timelessness. And as the poet said, the mind comes to rest, not in the head, but in the heart.

Having come to rest, we remember. It is not through intellection but through stillness that we remember. Remember. Re-member. To remember is to finally see how the apparent separation of reality actually fits together in a single wholeness. Discursive thought can only ever examine pieces of the whole. To re-member is to have the full vision of Wholeness, as things actually are. But this vision is found in timelessness and stillness, through the quiet mind unfiltered.

> And there is nothing left to say
> but we are That.
>
> And that is what we sing about.

—⁓—

174

Nirvana Shatakam

I am not mind, not intellect, not ego, not thought.
I am not the ears, the tongue, the nose or the eyes, or
    what they witness,
I am neither earth nor sky, not air or light.

I am knowledge and bliss.
I am Shiva! I am Shiva!

I am not the breath of prana, not its five currents.
I am not the seven elements, not the five organs,
Neither am I the voice nor hands nor anything that acts.

I am knowledge and bliss.
I am Shiva! I am Shiva!

I have no hatred or preference, neither greed nor desire
    nor delusion.
Pride, conflict, jealousy—these have no part of me.
Nothing do I own, nothing do I seek, not even
    liberation itself.

I am knowledge and bliss.
I am Shiva! I am Shiva!

I know neither virtue nor vice, neither pleasure nor
    pain.
I know no sacred chants, no holy places, no scriptures,
    no rituals.
I know neither the taste nor the taster.

I am knowledge and bliss.

I am Shiva! I am Shiva!

I fear not death. I doubt neither my being nor my place.
I have no father or mother; I am unborn.
I have no relatives, no friends. I have no guru and no
    devotees.

I am knowledge and bliss.
I am Shiva! I am Shiva!

Free from doubt, I am formless.
With knowledge, in knowledge, I am everywhere,
    beyond perception.
I am always the same. Not free, not trapped—I am.

I am knowledge and bliss.
I am Shiva! I am Shiva!

Truly, I am Shiva, pure awareness.
Shivo Ham! Shivo Ham!

Shankara

IMG

Nirvana Shatakam ～つ

This is one of the most important poems by the great Hindu philosopher-saint, Shankara. These lines are a distillation of *Advaita Vedanta*, the vision of non-dual reality. *Advaita* is the realization that underlying the complex diversity of creation is a single Unity. And within that Unity, even the individual is in no way separate or different from that vast Divine. This is why Shankara keeps returning to his refrain:

> *I am knowledge and bliss.*
> *I am Shiva! I am Shiva!*

You might ask, why Shiva? If all is One, why then identify with just one god from among the many gods in the Hindu pantheon?

Some schools of *Advaita Vedanta* do, in fact, avoid the theistic language of gods and, instead, speak only of the Self—the immense Self that is at once the heart of every individual and also the heart of all Being.

But when adherents of *Advaita* do speak of gods, they usually speak of Shiva. Shiva is the favored god of meditators, yogis, ascetics, those on the path of gnosis. Shiva is seen as pure Being, the fountain of all being. When Shankara repeats, "I am Shiva!" he is declaring that he finds no separation between his individual self and the center of all selves.

> *I am...*

Shankara asserts, "I am," throughout. By reading this poem, we repeat with him, "I am... I am..." Doing so, we enter into his realization. We take on his awareness. His declaration of what he is and is not becomes our own.

> *I am not mind, not intellect, not ego, not thought...*

Much of this poem is a list of what Shankara realizes we are not.

This is an expression of the ancient practice of *neti neti*—not this, not that. It is a spiritual examination of everything, while slowly recognizing that no single thing contains the full Reality we seek.

We are not the mind or intellect. We are not the senses or the organs through which we perceive the world. We are not the elemental building blocks of the body or the mind.

He also states we are not the qualities or preferences of the personality. The things that tug at us or repel us, they are not what we are, and they are not fundamentally real. Relationships, family, even life and death—none of these things define us or truly tell us who we are.

Shankara has basically negated everything: the body, the mind, desires and fears, relationships, even the hope for liberation itself. What then is left? That's the question that resonates throughout. Superficial ideas of identity would tell us that nothing remains and one has hit a dead end. Not so. Something remains. When all the rest has been swept aside, something remains. All the things you thought you were can be lost, yet you fundamentally remain. Beneath it all there has always been that glowing Self, steady, aware, at rest, blissful, invulnerable. And it says simply, "I am."

> Free from doubt, I am formless.
> With knowledge, in knowledge, I am everywhere, beyond
>   perception.
> I am always the same. Not free, not trapped—I am.

In celebration, we can sing with Shankara—

> I am knowledge and bliss.
> I am Shiva! I am Shiva!

> Truly, I am Shiva, pure awareness.
> Shivo Ham! Shivo Ham!

Buddha's body
accepts it…
winter rain

Issa

English version by David G. Lanoue

Buddha's body accepts it ∿

I could live on the nourishment of haiku every day. A few lines, so short they're almost incoherent. The way they teeter at the brink of meaning and occasionally slip into the void... Something about that desperate edge dares the mind to burst open with insight.

This haiku, for example—I don't read it as being about enduring uncomfortable weather. There is more than that here. There is acceptance, a quiet contentment, even a welcoming. It is about the recognition of the rightness of things in their season. And that touches the eternal.

The Buddha is here, always here, always present, and we feel the winter rain is simply passing by for its short moment. The rain touches the Buddha's face, and then moves on. So too the wind, the sun, the rising of grasses, the blooming of flowers. They come. The Buddha sits, smiles, accepts. And the world moves along again in its cycles of life, becoming and unbecoming, while the Buddha remains.

And what is the Buddha's body but us? The Buddha's body is our very nature. The physical body arises for a while and eventually declines. The seasons of the self blossom and turn inward again. Through it all there is a still point within us quietly watching, and accepting, and smiling.

—◠◡◠—

AFTERWORD

Through poetry the illuminated state becomes contagious.

Poetry has an immediate effect on the mind. The simple act of reading poetry alters thought patterns and the shuttle of the breath. Poetry induces trance. Its words are chant. Its rhythms are drumbeats. Its images become the icons of the inner eye. Sacred poetry is more than a description of the sacred experience; it carries the experience itself.

As you read these poems, may you too catch that igniting spark.

IMG

Glossary

Advaita   (Hinduism; "nondualism") *Advaita*, or *Advaita Vedanta*, is the metaphysical insight that everything is one, with no separation between mundane reality and divine reality. This implies that one is not separate from God, but that God is one's very nature as the true Self.

Awen   (Celtic, Welsh) *Awen* is both inspiration and spiritual power. It is the creative force that imbues all great art with life.

Chakra   (Hinduism; "wheel") The *chakras* are wheels of light within the energetic body. The primary *chakras* line up along the spine, from the seat to the crown of the head. Each *chakra* is associated with a color, a sound or vibration, a gland in the body, and specific psychological qualities. During spiritual emergence, the *Kundalini* (see below) rises through the primary *chakras* to the crown *chakra*, described as a thousand-petaled lotus and the seat of enlightened awareness.

Dervish   (Islam) A traveling ascetic and mystic. Some are hermits who have minimal interaction with society, while others inspire through teaching, stories, songs, even juggling.

Dharma   (Hinduism/Buddhism; also *dhamma*) *Dharma* can be broadly translated as "the right way." Its full meaning encompasses truth, law, rightness, spiritual practice, religious doctrine, and harmony.

Fana   (Islam; "annihilation") The state of ecstatic union between the soul and God in which the individual ego-self ceases to exist. (See also *samadhi*.)

Faqir   (Islam; also *fakir*) A Sufi ascetic, an itinerant Muslim holy beggar, a wandering *dervish*.

Hajj   (Islam) The *Hajj* is the holy pilgrimage to Mecca, which should be performed at least once in a Muslim's life, if it is feasible. In centuries past, when travel was much more difficult, the pilgrimage was often an arduous, lengthy, life-defining journey that allowed the devout to learn wisdom from many spiritual teachers along the way while gaining a wider understanding of humanity and the world.

Ho'oponopono   (Hawaiian; see also *pono*) A traditional Hawaiian healing practice that works with groups of people: families,

184

communities, culture. The word *ho'oponopono* means "to make things right" or "to reestablish harmony."

Ishwara   (Hinduism; "lord") A reference to God, much as Lord is used in Judeo-Christian language. The term implies a highly personal attachment to the particular form of God, as the lord of one's heart.

Japa   (Hinduism; see also *mantra*) Similar to the practice of *mantra* yoga, involving the chanting of spiritually empowered sounds. The emphasis in *japa*, however, is on repetition. In *japa*, the *mantra* is repeated to such an extent that the mind ceases its normal inattentive chatter and grows silent, allowing true meditation to occur.

Karma   (Hinduism/Buddhism; "action") In spiritual terms, *karma* is the universal law that every action magnetically draws an energetic result. These energetic *karmas* act as seeds, which, at the right time, mature into new experiences that are either pleasant or unpleasant, depending on the original action. (This is similar to Christ's teaching that "as ye sow, so shall ye reap.") Much of Hindu and Buddhist philosophy is focused on ways to free the individual from this seemingly endless cycle of action and reaction.

Koan   (Buddhism/Zen) A riddle-like question or statement without an obvious answer. The Zen student meditates on a *koan* in order to bypass the mind's limitations and thus attain insight and enlightenment.

Kundalini   (Hinduism) In yoga, the *Kundalini* is the fundamental spiritual energy, typically dormant at the base of the spine. When, through spiritual practice, the fiery *Kundalini* is roused, it rises up the spine to the crown. This can lead to bliss, egolessness, and enlightenment.

Mahasamadhi(Hinduism; "supreme *samadhi*"—see also *samadhi*) This is the term usually applied to the death of a saintly figure in Hinduism, implying conscious exit from the physical body and complete union with the Divine.

Maitreya   (Buddhism) A future Buddha predicted to appear in order to bring enlightenment when the world has fallen into darkness. The Maitreya Buddha can be compared in some ways to Judeo-Christian ideas of the Messiah.

Mantra	(Hinduism /Buddhism) A spiritually empowered sound or statement, often proclaiming the divine nature of reality and the individual's relationship to or identification with God. This can be chanted or sung in order to settle the heart, focus the mind, and cultivate spiritual opening within the individual.
Mi'raj	(Islam) The sacred journey of the Prophet Mohammed in which he ascended from Jerusalem through the seven heavens, conversed with heavenly prophets, and drew near to the throne of God.
Neti Neti	(Hinduism; "not this, not that") This is a reference to the yogic spiritual practice of negation, in which every aspect of life is examined and recognized to be short of the spiritual goal. This helps the practitioner to be free from false identification and limiting attachment in order to better see the true goal, which is all-encompassing and, therefore, never fully contained in any single object, person or experience.
Pono	(Hawaiian; "rightness" or "harmony") In Hawaiian culture, a situation is said to be *pono* when justice or balance has been restored.
Prana	(Hinduism; "life") *Prana* is the subtle life force that pervades the universe and vivifies living beings. When *prana* flows unhindered through the channels of the energetic body, the individual may experience greater health or become open to enlightenment. *Prana* is intimately linked with the breath; thus breathing techniques are an important part of many yogic practices.
Qigong	(Taoism; also *chi kung*) Practices to cultivate and direct chi, subtle energies used by body and spirit for well-being. *Qigong* practice involves slow fluid movement, attentive breathing, and meditative states of mind.
Samadhi	(Hinduism/Buddhism) The conscious merging of the individual awareness with the Eternal. This state is one of profound stillness, mental quiet, ecstatic bliss, and freedom from the idea of an egoic self.
Sangha	(Hinduism/Buddhism) Spiritual community, the fellowship of devotees and practitioners.
Satori	(Japanese Buddhism; "understanding") Particularly emphasized in Zen Buddhism, *satori* is the profound flash of insight or

enlightenment that occurs when the meditator suddenly recognizes the true nature of reality.

Shakti
(Hinduism; "power") The feminine expression of God in the form of divine power, vibration, and manifestation. Shakti is understood on several levels, as spiritual energy, as the vibrational energy that underlies all creation, as creation itself, and as the living Goddess. Often Shakti is paired with Shiva to suggest the masculine and feminine unified within the supreme expression of God.

Shiva
(Hinduism) This Hindu god is especially associated with yogic and ascetic practices. Many devotees relate to Shiva as the ultimate transcendent Reality. Other times Shiva is portrayed as the masculine aspect of God, paired with Shakti or another Hindu goddess. Other metaphysical formulations see him as one of the trinity of major gods: Brahma (creator), Vishnu (preserver), and Shiva (destroyer, transformer).

Sufi
(Islam) A follower of Sufism, a Muslim mystic (see below).

Sufism
(Islam) An esoteric expression of Islam. Many different schools and lineages exist among Sufis, usually tracing their origin to one of the great figures of early Islam. Some practices emphasize asceticism and itinerancy ("wandering *dervishes*"), while others focus on elevated philosophy or emphasize losing one's self in the love of God.

Tao
(Taoism) The Tao is the unnamable absolute Reality underlying all of existence. Often the word Tao is translated as "the Way," but this way is not so much a tradition or code of behavior as the inherent nature of self and being. The Tao divides itself into yin and yang, the balanced principles of feminine and masculine energies from which all of manifest reality emerges.

Yoga
(Hinduism; "union") An ancient body of practices, traditions, and philosophies within esoteric Hinduism leading the individual to enlightenment, freedom from the wheel of *karma*, and conscious union with the Divine.

Zikr
(Islam; "remembrance"—also *dhikr*) A Muslim spiritual practice, particularly among Sufis, of repeating, chanting, or singing the names of God and other sacred phrases, often in all-night gatherings.

About the Poets

Abu-Said Abil-Kheir (Turkmenistan, 967 – 1049)

Shaikh Abu-Said Abil-Kheir was a Sufi who famously referred to himself as "Nobody, Son of Nobody" to convey the mystic's sense of having merged with the Divine, leaving no trace of the ego behind. He lived in what is modern day Turkmenistan, just north of Iran and Afghanistan in Central Asia.

AE (George William Russell) (Ireland, 1867 – 1935)

George William Russell was an Irish nationalist and activist, an essayist, a poet, a painter, and a mystic. Russell was a close friend of his contemporary, W. B. Yeats. As with many spiritual-minded people of his era, he was a theosophist, interested in clairvoyance and Eastern mysticism. He adopted his pen name "AE" for Aeon, to suggest a new era of the human spirit.

Hogan Bays (United States, 1949 –)

Zen Teacher Hogan Bays is co-abbot of the Great Vow Zen Monastery in Oregon. He began his Zen practice in 1968, studying with Philip Kapleau, Roshi. Since 1990, he has studied with Shodo Harada, Roshi. Hogan Bays worked for the Oregon Department of Corrections for 15 years.

William Blake (England, 1757 – 1827)

William Blake was a poet, artist, and visionary of eccentric genius. He married in his mid 20s and supported himself by doing engravings, etchings, and illustrations. It was also during this period that he published his first works of poetry. Blake was a progressive social thinker and inclined to clash with authority. Throughout his life Blake had visions and believed that archangels guided him in his art. Much of his strongest work took on a prophetic quality. Although his spirituality was deeply inspired by the Bible and Christianity, he was a vocal critic of narrow-minded religiosity. Blake famously wrote, "If the doors of perception were cleansed every thing would appear to man as it is, infinite." His work has been an important influence among Romantic poets, artists, social critics, and visionary seekers.

Bulleh Shah (Pakistan/India, 1680 – 1758)

As a young man, Bulleh Shah was a respected scholar, but his longing for true realization led him to the Sufi path, over the objections of his peers. Bulleh Shah's realization led to such profound egolessness that all concern for social convention fell away. His 'foolish wisdom' is the source of many comic tales that cut through social propriety in order to reveal underlying truths. Bulleh Shah is one of the most revered mystic poets of the Punjab region.

Andrew Colliver (Australia, 1953 –)

Andrew Colliver is a psychiatric social worker living in rural New South Wales in Australia. He writes, "In 2006, the experience—now happening to thousands across the globe—of consciousness awakening to itself within the human form, began to up-end my life, and also to seek expression in words. Ideas and words come most frequently when I'm in nature, but any setting can be seen at any time for what it is: the expression of undivided consciousness."

Emily Dickinson (United States, 1830 – 1886)

Emily Dickinson was born to a prominent family in Amherst, Massachusetts. Despite literary anonymity during her lifetime, Dickinson has come to be regarded as one of the greatest of American poets. Her unusual use of rhyme, meter, and grammar anticipates modern poetic trends. Dickinson was a critic of the common practice of religion in her day, yet she experienced a rich inner life that she understood in religious terms. Much of her poetry meditates on heaven and the inner life, often contrasting the private moment against religious convention. If one reads her poetry side-by-side with the poet-saints of India and elsewhere, the parallels in metaphoric language and insight are striking. Much is made of Dickinson's reclusive life, the fact that she never married, and the focus on death in her poetry, leading to characterizations of her as a morbid, sexually repressed recluse. Recognizing the depth of her inner life, however, we can also view her as an urban hermit and contemplative poet.

Yunus Emre (Turkey, 1238 – 1320)

Yunus Emre and Rumi were contemporaries, both living in the same general region. But while Rumi lived and taught among the well-educated urban Sufi circles and wrote primarily in Persian, Yunus Emre traveled among the rural poor, singing his songs in the Turkish language of the common people.

Francis of Assisi (Italy, 1181 – 1226)

St. Francis was born to a prosperous merchant family in Assisi, Italy. As a youth he led a raucous, high-spirited life but, after an aborted attempt to join the Crusades, Francis turned inward, devoting his time to prayer, solitude in nature, and service to the sick and the poor. Followers quickly gathered about him. He navigated a careful path, maintaining his essential message of service, poverty, and introversion, while avoiding overt criticism of Church excesses. Francis famously received the stigmata, Christ's wounds, while praying among a group of caves in the countryside. He died in 1226 at the age of 45 and was immediately acclaimed to be a saint by the general population.

George Herbert (Wales & England, 1593 – 1633)

Though born to a wealthy family, George Herbert lived the humble life of a country clergyman. The quiet service he offered to his parish earned him the nickname "Holy Mr. Herbert." His poetry was not published until after his death, but quickly became an important influence within the religious and spiritual life of the country.

Issa (Japan, 1763 – 1828)

Kobayashi Nobuyuki was a lay Buddhist priest and one of the great haiku masters. He adopted the pen name Issa, which means "a single cup of tea." Although Issa's life was filled with struggles—the death of his mother at an early age, conflicts with his stepmother, poverty, and the death of his own children— his haiku tend to celebrate the serenity of simple spiritual moments in life.

John of the Cross (Spain, 1542 – 1591)

John of the Cross was raised in poverty by his widowed mother. In his early 20s, he entered the Carmelite Order and soon after met the woman who would become his mentor, Teresa of Avila. Teresa of Avila had begun a reform movement within their monastic order, advocating a return to simplicity and essential spirituality. John of the Cross joined her Discalced Carmelites and quickly became a leading figure within the movement. Other Carmelites felt threatened by the new movement, and they turned to force, capturing and imprisoning John of the Cross. It was in prison that John began to write poetry on smuggled scraps of paper. He escaped after nine months of imprisonment. John spent the rest of his life as a spiritual director among the Discalced Carmelites. His two best known works, the *Spiritual Canticle* and *Dark Night of the Soul*, are considered masterpieces of Spanish poetry and esoteric Christianity.

Kabir (India, 1440? – 1518)

Kabir is not easily categorized as a Sufi or a yogi—he is both of these and more. Today, he is revered by Muslims, Hindus, and Sikhs alike. He was born in Varanasi (Benares) to Muslim parents. Early in his life Kabir became a disciple of the Hindu *bhakti* saint Ramananda. Kabir never abandoned worldly life, choosing instead to live the balanced life of a householder and mystic, tradesman and contemplative. Kabir was married, had children, and worked as a weaver. The end of his life was spent in exile for his criticism of religious and secular authorities. One of the most loved legends associated with Kabir is told of his funeral. Kabir's disciples disputed over his body, the Muslims wanting to bury the body, the Hindus wanting its cremation. Kabir appeared to the arguing disciples and told them to lift the burial shroud. When they did so, they found fragrant flowers where the body had rested. The flowers were divided, and the Muslims buried the flowers while the Hindus reverently committed them to fire.

Edith Kanaka'ole (Hawaii, 1913 – 1979)

Edith Kekuhikuhipu'uoneo'naali'iokohala Kanaka'ole was a *kumu hula* (master hula teacher), respected Hawaiian *kupuna* (elder), and teacher of Hawaiian Studies at the University of Hawaii at Hilo.

Omar Khayyam (Persia/Iran, 1048 – 1131)

Omar Khayyam was a mathematician and astronomer. His quatrains (or *rubaiyat*) are commonly read in the West as a collection of sensual love poems. Although the question is still debated, Persian tradition asserts that Khayyam was a Sufi and his *Rubaiyat* can only be properly understood as spiritual metaphor.

Baba Kuhi of Shiraz (Persia/Iran, 980? – 1050)

Baba Kuhi spent years in retreat in a mountain cave north of Shiraz, Iran. It is said that before Baba Kuhi died, he proclaimed that whoever could stay awake for forty consecutive nights at his tomb would be granted the gift of poetry and his heart's desire. The later Sufi poet Hafiz, recalling the famous 'promise of Baba Kuhi,' kept the vigil to gain the love of a woman. Finally, utterly exhausted, Hafiz saw a shining angel who asked him what he desired most. Hafiz was so dazzled by the sight of the angel that he forgot about the young woman and declared only that he wanted God.

Lalla (Kashmir/India/Pakistan, 14th century)

Little is known for certain about the life of Lalla (or Lal Ded), other than hints that come to us through her poetry and songs. Tradition says she was a young bride forced into an unhappy marriage and abused by her husband's family. Still in her early 20s, she left the marriage and took up the life of a wandering holy woman, singing songs of enlightenment to her beloved god Shiva.

Stephen Levine (United States, 1937 –)
Stephen Levine is the author of several classic books in the field of conscious living and dying. His poetry reflects a deep attention, and an appreciation for the opportunities of self-awareness as we approach that unavoidable mystery, death.

Li Bai (China, 701 – 762)
Li Bai (or Li Po) was raised in Szechwan in western China. In his 40s, he was appointed to a high academy position, but he was later exiled for political reasons. He then worked in the service of a southern prince who rose up in rebellion. Li Bai was exiled a second time, but pardoned. Li Bai's poetry is particularly known for its elegance. It suggests a certain serene poise and quietness of mind.

Antonio Machado (Spain, 1763 – 1828)
Antonio Machado's poetry discovers revelation in the rural landscape and in the yearning of the human heart. Machado's wife died when she was very young. His lifelong anguish over this loss enters his poetry as a sort of private communion. His wife is ever with him, yet just out of reach, beckoning him to deeper awareness.

Akka Mahadevi (India, 12th century)
Akka Mahadevi escaped an arranged marriage to live as a wandering holy woman and poet, singing praises to Lord Shiva. A true ascetic, Mahadevi refused to wear clothes—a common practice among male ascetics, but shocking for a woman. Tradition says she chose a conscious exit from the world in her twenties, entering *mahasamadhi* (final divine union) with a flash of light.

Navajo Prayer (North America)
The traditional lands of the Navajo are in northern Arizona, New Mexico, southern Colorado, and Utah.

Colin Oliver (England, 1946 –)
Colin Oliver lives with his wife in a rural community in England. He says of his writing, "Many of my poems are directly expressive of seeing into that transparent inner nature which I believe we all share but so often overlook."

Pima Medicine Man's Song (North America)
The Pima are a native people whose traditional homelands are in Arizona.

Jay Ramsay (England, 1958 –)
Jay Ramsay is a British poet, translator, and psychotherapist. His poetry is a voice for transformative spiritual, political, and psychological awareness.

Elizabeth Reninger (United States, 1963 –)
Elizabeth Reninger is a poet, and a practitioner of yoga, as well as the Taoist arts of *qigong*, acupuncture, and *tuina*. She has been exploring the terrain of Inner Alchemy in various forms for upwards of twenty-five years.

Mevlana Jelaluddin Rumi (Persia/Afghanistan & Turkey, 1207 – 1273)

Rumi was born in the eastern end of the Persian Empire in what is today Afghanistan. While he was still a boy, his family fled the Mongol invasion and settled in Asia Minor (Turkey). Rumi was already a man with religious position when he encountered the wandering *dervish* Shams, who became his spiritual teacher. This meeting ignited a spiritual revolution within Rumi, his community, his poetry… a revolution that reaches into the present day.

Ryokan (Japan, 1758 – 1831)

Ryokan became a Zen priest at 18. After a period of wandering, he settled down to study meditation. When his teacher died, Ryokan inherited leadership of the temple. But the duties and regularity of being temple master didn't suit Ryokan, and he resumed the life of an itinerant monk. Ryokan's gentleness and playful nature are often reflected in his poems and the stories told about him.

Hakim Sanai (Afghanistan, 1044? – 1150?)

The story is told that the Sultan of Ghazna decided to invade neighboring India, and Sanai, as court poet, was summoned to record his exploits. Passing by a garden, he heard a notorious drunk toasting the foolishness of both the sultan and his young poet. Struck by these words, Sanai abandoned his pampered life, became a Sufi, and went on pilgrimage to distant Mecca, composing his masterpiece of spiritual poetry, *The Walled Garden of Truth*.

Sarmad (Persia/Iran & India, 17th century)

Sarmad was born to a merchant family that may have been Jewish. He traveled from Persia to India, abandoning the life of a merchant for that of a naked *faqir*. Sarmad became a vocal critic of arbitrary political and religious power, leading to his execution for unorthodoxy. Sarmad was loved by the people, and his death triggered riots. Today, his tomb is visited by people of all faiths.

Sachal Sarmast (Pakistan/India, 1739 – 1829)

Sachal Sarmast lived a humble, ascetic life, preferring solitude and simple meals of *dhal* and yogurt. It is said he never left the village of his birth, yet he composed sacred poetry in multiple languages. The name he took, Sachal, means "Truth." Later devotees added Sarmast, meaning "Ecstatic Master."

Shabistari (Persia/Iran, 1250? – 1340)

Mahmud Shabistari lived in Persia (Iran) during the time of the Mongol invasions. It was a terrible time of massacres, yet it is also during this time that the Golden Age of Persian Sufism emerged. Shabistari's *Secret Rose Garden* is considered to be one of the finest works of Persian Sufism. His poetry expresses a unified vision of reality within the elegant language of the Persian poetic tradition.

Shankara (India, 788 – 820)

Shankara (Adi Shankara or Shankaracharya) was an immensely important philosopher, sage, holy man, and poet who, more than any other figure, unified Hinduism's nondualist *Advaita* teachings into an essential philosophical tradition. Shankara left home at a young age to seek a guru and receive initiation into monastic life. Later in life, he traveled extensively, engaging in philosophical debates while strengthening ideas of nondualism within Hindu thought. Many Hindu monastic lineages trace their roots back to Adi Shankaracharya as their founder.

Angelus Silesius (Poland & Germany, 1624 – 1677)
Angelus Silesius was born into a noble Polish Lutheran family. Frustrated by the rigid Lutheranism of his era, he converted to Catholicism. He was briefly physician to the Holy Roman Emperor but soon became a monk and priest, giving away his family fortune to the needy. Today, his poems are loved by both Catholics and Protestants.

Vladimir Solovyov (Russia, 1853 – 1900)
Vladimir Sergeyevich Solovyov (or Soloviev) was an influential philosopher, poet, literary critic, and mystic with an intense connection to the divine female archetype, Sophia or Holy Wisdom. Solovyov was friends with many great artists and writers, including the Russian novelist, Fyodor Dostoevsky.

Symeon the New Theologian (Byzantine Empire/Turkey, 949 – 1032)
Symeon was born into an aristocratic family and, as a young man, he rose to the post of imperial senator. Yet his public life was in conflict with his inner life. Symeon left the senate and became a monk and a priest, eventually taking on the role of abbot. The mystical practices he advocated led to conflicts with church authorities, but eager students flocked to him. Today, he is one of the most important spiritual figures of the Eastern Orthodox Church.

Rabindranath Tagore (India, 1861 – 1941)
Rabindranath Tagore was born to a wealthy Brahmin family in Calcutta (Kolkata) in West Bengal during the British occupation of India. Tagore's mother died when he was a young child and his father was often away, leaving Rabindranath to be raised by elder siblings and family servants. His family was central to regional political, intellectual, and artistic social circles, ensuring that the young Tagore was exposed to great art and learning from an early age. During his lifetime, Tagore traveled extensively, meeting the world's great writers, scientists, political leaders, and social reformers. Tagore's poetry draws from the rich devotional poetic traditions of India, but is expressed in a highly fluid, contemporary style. His impact on world poetry and literature is immense. Although his poetic writings are extensive, Tagore's most known and loved collection is *Gitanjali* (or *Song Offerings*). In 1913, Rabindranath Tagore became the first non-European to win the Nobel Prize in Literature.

Alfred Lord Tennyson (England, 1809 – 1892)
Despite a troubled upbringing and periods of extreme poverty as a young man, Alfred Tennyson experienced ecstatic states that he described as "a kind of waking trance... The individuality itself seemed to dissolve and fade away into boundless being, and this not a confused state but the clearest, the surest of the surest... utterly beyond words—where death was an almost laughable impossibility, the loss of personality (if so it were) seeming no extinction, but the only true life." His poetry gained fame and access to higher social circles, leading

to a lordship and the post of Britain's Poet Laureate during the reign of Queen Victoria.

Teresa of Avila (Spain, 1515 – 1582)
Teresa of Avila was a Catholic nun, spiritual leader, and saint. She led the Discalced Carmelites, a reform movement that advocated simplicity and the spiritual life in contrast to the worldly and sometimes corrupt practices of many monastic orders. She wrote poetry, letters, and histories, but it is her book on the path of prayer, *The Way of Perfection*, and her spiritual autobiography, *The Interior Castle*, that are considered her masterpieces.

Thomas Traherne (England, 1636? – 1674)
Despite being an agnostic, Traherne took up the life of a small town clergyman. But while still a young man, he went through a transformative mystical experience and sought to express his new "Felicity" through writing, most of which remained unpublished until more than 200 years after his death.

Henry Vaughan (Wales, 1621 – 1695)
Amidst the English Civil War, Vaughan had a powerful mystical conversion, which he links to the inspired poetry of George Herbert. But, in contrast to Herbert's praises, Vaughan was more immediate and overtly mystical in his writing. His poetry describes ecstatic states of divine communion and a deep affinity for the natural world. Vaughan became a respected physician, collecting his metaphysical poetry as *Silex Scintillus* (The Fiery Flint).

Dorothy Walters (United States, 1928 –)
Dorothy Walters, Ph.D., helped to set up one of the first women's studies programs in the country and was active in the early feminist and gay liberation movements. In 1981 she experienced a dramatic spiritual transformation through spontaneous *Kundalini* awakening. Since then, she has focused on writing about the spiritual journey, while helping to guide others who are undergoing similar experiences of transformation.

Walt Whitman (United States, 1819 – 1892)
Walt Whitman grew up in Brooklyn and Long Island. He trained as a printer from the age of twelve. He learned to love the written word and read all he could. In his late teens he became a teacher, then turned to journalism in his 20s, briefly moving to New Orleans as editor of a local newspaper. Having witnessed the cruelties of slavery in the South, he returned to Brooklyn as a confirmed abolitionist. Whitman self-published the first edition of what would come to be seen as his masterpiece, *Leaves of Grass*, in 1855, revising it several times in subsequent years. During the Civil War, Walt Whitman worked as a reporter and aided the wounded in local hospitals. Whitman struggled financially for many years, but with the successful publication of the 1882 edition of *Leaves of Grass* he finally began to earn enough money to purchase a house and live comfortably through his final years.

William Wordsworth (England, 1770 – 1850)

The Romantic poetry of William Wordsworth discovers meditative insights and transcendence amidst the natural world. Wordsworth was born to a prosperous family in the scenic Lake District of northwest England. His mother died while he was still a child. Prior to graduation from Cambridge, Wordsworth took a walking tour of Europe, reveling in the beauty of the Alps. Among his most loved poems are "Tintern Abbey," "Ode: Intimations of Immortality from Recollections of Early Childhood," and "The Prelude." In 1843 Wordsworth was named England's Poet Laureate.

Yamei (Japan, 1662? – 1713)

In addition to being a poet, Sakai Yamei was a *ronin* (a masterless samurai). Originally from the southern island of Kyushu, he later settled in Kyoto. He received the haiku name, Yamei, from the great haiku poet, Matsuo Basho.

Hsu Yun (China, 1839 – 1959)

The Venerable Master Hsu Yun was born in 1839 or 1840 in the Guanzhou region of China. At the age of 20, Hsu Yun went against his father's wishes and became an ordained monk. He had a naturally ascetic temperament and often refused even the minimal food of a monk. Hsu Yun traveled and taught in many parts of China and Southeast Asia. He is credited by many with revitalizing Buddhist practice throughout much of the region, which was showing signs of degeneration and decline in the period leading up to and following the communist revolution. Although he was greatly respected, Hsu Yun remained supremely humble and simple in his lifestyle. He chose to live the final years of his long life quietly in his monastery's cow shed.

Acknowledgments

I wish to sincerely thank everyone who helped me to complete this anthology:

My wife, Michele Anderson, for her love, encouragement, and adventurous spirit.

Danny Mack, for providing a flexible and creative work environment, allowing this misfit poet to support his family while bringing these meditations to print.

Aparna Sharma, for her excellent editorial suggestions, vision, and practical focus in preparing the manuscript that would eventually become the book you hold.

My international band of keen-eyed proofreaders. Your diligence, patience, and willingness to mark up my manuscript helped more than I can say.

The entire Poetry Chaikhana community, for your wise, touching, and often witty responses to my many emails and blog posts over the years. Your enthusiastic feedback is an important reason why this book exists today.

Thanks also to the following poets, translators, and publishers for their generous permission to include their work in this collection.

Abu-Said Abil-Kheir, "Love came and emptied me of self" English version by Vraje Abramian. Originally published in *Nobody, Son of Nobody: Poems of Shaikh Abu-Saeed Abil-Kheir* (Hohm Press). Used by permission of the publisher.

Hogan Bays, "Liberation From All Obstructions" Chanted daily at the Great Vow Zen Monastery in Oregon. Written in appreciation of Shodo Harada, Roshi. Used by permission of the author.

Bulleh Shah, "One Thread Only" English version by Ivan M. Granger. Originally published in *Real Thirst: Poetry of the Spiritual Journey* (Poetry Chaikhana). "Chanting the Beloved's name" English version by Ivan M. Granger.

Andrew Colliver, "The Further You Go" Used by permission of the author.

Yunus Emre, "The way of the masters" Translated by Kabir Helminski and Refik Algan. Originally published in *The Drop that Became the Sea: Lyric Poems of Yunus Emre* (Threshold). Reprinted by permission of Kabir Helminski.

Francis of Assisi "The Canticle of Brother Sun" English version by Ivan M. Granger.

Issa, "Even poorly planted" and "Buddha's body accepts it" Translated by David G. Lanoue. Originally published on The Haiku of Kobayashi Issa website *www.haikuguy.com/issa/*. Used by permission of David G. Lanoue. "Mountains" English version by Ivan M. Granger.

John of the Cross, "Love's Living Flame" Translation by Ivan M. Granger.

Kabir, "My body is flooded" English version by Andrew Harvey. Originally published in *Perfume of the Desert: Inspirations from Sufi Wisdom* (Quest Books). Used by permission of Andrew Harvey.

Edith Kanaka'ole, "E Ho Mai" Copyright The Edith Kanaka'ole Foundation (Hilo, HI). Reprinted with the kind permission of the author's daughter, Pualani Kanahele.

Lalla, "One shrine to the next" Translated by Ranjit Hoskote. Originally published in *I, Lalla: The Poems of Lal Ded* (Penguin Classics). Used by permission of Ranjit Hoskote. "Learning the scriptures is easy" English version by Ivan M. Granger.

Stephen Levine, "Millennium Blessing" Originally published in *Breaking the Drought: Visions of Grace* (Larson Publications). Used by permission of the author.

Li Bai, "Sitting (Reverence Mountain)" Translated by Doug Westendorp. Originally published in *I Take Your Poems to the Mountains: Poems and Translations from Tang Dynasty China.* Used by permission of Doug Westendorp.

Antonio Machado, "Last night, as I was sleeping" Translation by Ivan M. Granger.

Akka Mahadevi, "You are all the forest" and "Like a river in flood" English versions by Ivan M. Granger.

Colin Oliver, "Boundless" Originally published in *Stepping Into Brilliant Air* (The Shollond Trust). Also published in *Nothing but this Moment* ebook (The Shollond Trust). Used by permission of the author.

"Pima Medicine Man's Song" English version by Brian Swann. Originally published in *Song of the Sky: Versions of Native American Song-Poems* (University of Massachusetts Press). Adapted from George Herzog/JAF . Used by permission of Brian Swann.

Jay Ramsay, "I saw a great light" Originally published in *Transmissions* (Stride Publications). Used by permission of the author.

Elizabeth Reninger, "Bird Bath" Originally published in *And Now the Story Lives Inside You* (Woven Word Press). Used by permission of the author.

Gabriel Rosenstock, "a star" Used by permission of the author.

Mevlana Jelaluddin Rumi, "Not only do the thirsty seek water" English version by Ivan M. Granger. "The Absolute works with nothing" Excerpted from "Be Like Melting Snow." English version © Coleman Barks. Originally published in *The Essential Rumi* (HarperOne). Reprinted by permission of Coleman Barks. "I lost my world my fame my mind" English version by Andrew Harvey. Originally published in *The Way of Passion: A Celebration of Rumi* (Tarcher). Reprinted by permission of Andrew Harvey.

Ryokan, "Thinking" English version by Gabriel Rosenstock. Originally published in *Haiku: The Gentle Art of Disappearing* (Cambridge Scholars Publishing). Used by permission of Gabriel Rosenstock.

Hakim Sanai, "Bring all of yourself" and "Belief and learning led the way" English versions by Ivan M. Granger. "There is no place for place" English version by Ivan M. Granger. Originally published in *Real Thirst: Poetry of the Spiritual Journey* (Poetry Chaikhana).

Sarmad, "Every man who knows his secret" English version by Ivan M. Granger. Originally published in *Real Thirst: Poetry of the Spiritual Journey* (Poetry Chaikhana).

Sachal Sarmast, "Friend, this is the only way" English version by Ivan M. Granger. Originally published in *Real Thirst: Poetry of the Spiritual Journey* (Poetry Chaikhana).

Shankara, "Nirvana Shatakam" English version by Ivan M. Granger.

Angelus Silesius, "God, whose love and joy are present everywhere" Translated by Gabriel Rosenstock, from *Haiku: The Gentle Art of Disappearing* (Cambridge Scholars Publishing). Used by permission of Gabriel Rosenstock.

Vladimir Solovyov, "Sophia in Egypt" Excerpt from "Three Meetings." Translation by Ivan M. Granger. Originally published in *Real Thirst: Poetry of the Spiritual Journey* (Poetry Chaikhana).

Symeon the New Theologian, "How is it I can love You" and "The Light of Your Way" English versions by Ivan M. Granger. Originally published in *Real Thirst: Poetry of the Spiritual Journey* (Poetry Chaikhana).

Teresa of Avila, "On Those Words 'I am for My Beloved'" Translated by Megan Don, author of *Meditations with Teresa of Avila: A Journey into the Sacred* (New World Library). This translation is from her website *GnosticGrace.com*. Used by permission of Megan Don.

Dorothy Walters, "Waiting" Originally published in *Marrow of the Flame: Poems of the Spiritual Journey* (Hohm Press). Used by permission of the author.

Yamei, "Swallowing the open field" English version by Ivan M. Granger.

Hsu Yun, "An Exquisite Truth" English version by The Zen Buddhist Order of Hsu Yun. Used by permission.